500
HOME
BUSINESS
IDEAS

WOLFGANG RIEBE

First Published as 450 Home Business Ideas in 2009
Complete Revision & Upgrade to 500 Home Business Ideas in 2013

Publisher:
MindPower Publications
www.mindpowerpublications.com

Layout, Drawings & Cover Design: Elof Gribwagen

ISBN: 978-1479312191

**Many more inspirational books available at
the end of this book and at** www.wolfgangriebe.com
and hundreds of free videos at https://www.youtube.com/
inspiringtheworld

Creative commons cover photo courtesy of www.pixabay.com

CHAPTERS

FOREWORD

Welcome to 500 Home Business Ideas!

Much research has gone into finding practical and realistic ideas that will hopefully appeal to a broad range of people. I have really tried to give a fair spectrum of suggestions and trust that you will be able to find at least one good idea out of the five hundred. If not, let these ideas at least stimulate your mind to think about some business ventures of your own, or even come up with a combination of ideas. Remember, not all ideas are going to be up your alley, but even if only one idea is; that's money really well spent! The book has also been divided into ten chapters of 50 ideas each, thus making it easier for you to identify your areas of interest.

In all fairness you also need to realise that there are no 'secret' magic formula ideas out there. For the majority of people on this earth good honest hard work is what pays. If you bought this book expecting a 'Million Dollar' idea, and discovering the next 'Get Rich Quick' scheme where you can sit on your butt and watch the money roll in; dare I suggest you were maybe just a touch naïve?

Don't get me wrong; there are most definitely 'Million Dollar' ideas in this book. However, the reality is that only a select few people will see the opportunity and actually make the effort to do something with them. Are you going to be the one that does? Or are you going to continue to make excuses in life and blame others for your failures? Think of any profession... most people make a living and less than one percent are usually hugely successful. Yet it's the same profession in the same area with the same education; what makes that one person so different from the others? It's called attitude! Your attitude will determine the value of this book to you! I do believe that if you find an idea in these pages that you can 'connect' with, and are passionate about it, you have won half the battle. Of course you also need to deliver an exceptional service, and be professional in your dealings with all your clients; then there is no reason why you cannot build up a million dollar business in the long term.

Furthermore, please remember that these are ideas only! The title of the booklet says, 'Ideas.' Not business plans, strategies and complete business models, but ideas! Much of your success will rely on your attitude, service delivery and business skills. The aim of this book is to plant the seeds in your mind. It is up to you whether you water them and make these ideas grow! I therefore strongly suggest that you read up or attend a few courses on business skills so as to give you that edge.

Lastly, I can tweak your interest and give you the ideas only. What you do with them is up to you! As a speaker and a trainer I always like to make people think and see the positive side of any situation. Thus I would like you to consider the following question; if a successful forward thinking man like Sir Richard Branson (The man with the Virgin brand) were to tackle any one of the ideas in this book, do you think he would make a success of it or not? I would put money on it that he would!

Why? It's his attitude and his business skills!

So, what is stopping you?

Go for it!

ADMINISTRATIVE HOME BUSINESS IDEAS

50 Home Business Ideas you can literally do in your pyjamas! Yes here are 50 ideas covering a wide range of fields and topics. They are mainly administrative style ideas that you can run from your home. In other words, ideas that involve paperwork, admin, computer work and related fields and that you could in essence do in your pyjamas, in the comfort of your own home.

1. ADULT STORIES

Granted, this is not the best way to start 50 ideas and push sex as a topic. However, alphabetically, it starts with A, and there may well be people out there that have a knack, plus fertile imagination that makes it easy for them to come up with creative stories and ideas around adult themes and topics. Although rumour has it that sex is no longer the number one use of the Internet anymore, the adult industry is huge and many sites, magazines, online E-zines etc are always looking for adult stories and they pay well for these. If this is up your alley, approach various publications and do a search on the Internet. Of course you could even put together your own E-book of stories and market it on the Internet yourself. Before you criticise the idea, just look at the mega success of the mother of two, E.L. James with '50 Shades of Grey'!

2. BOOKKEEPER AND/OR TAX ASSISTANT

There are many small businesses that need the services of a good bookkeeper. Chartered accountants charge a steep hourly fee for their bookkeeping services. This means you should have no trouble finding work, if your rates are more reasonable that that of the big firms. If this interests you, but you have no experience, then consider taking a part time courses. There are many on offer at very reasonable rates and very soon you should be able to keep simple records, balance the books and fill in tax returns. If you don't want to do a course, but have good organisational skills, offer to sort and file invoices and all tax related documents for accountants and bookkeepers from home. The most time consuming part for many of these professionals is the sorting out in date order of business papers, as well as into groups, i.e. fuel, food, insurance payments, etc. This could be the start of a good business.

3. BANKRUPT STOCK/JOB LOTS OF EX-CATALOGUE GOODS - BUY AND SELL

Most start-up companies don't last for more than a year. What happens to all their unused stock, goods and products they still own? Here is an opportunity for you to source such companies and offer to sell these items for them on a commission basis per item, or for a set fee. If you are someone with contacts and enjoy networking with people, here is an opportunity to make really good money. You can initially visit auction houses and also contact banks to find out which companies are going into liquidation. All you then do is put the right people in touch with each other and play the middleman... for a fee!

4. BUY AND SELL ON THE INTERNET

Basically you offer to buy and sell anything and everything on the Internet - from upcoming artists' paintings to used cars. You have sites such as e-Bay where you can sell and source items. You may have a large social network and offer to sell stuff for them at a commission. The sky is the limit. You can do this from a home office and handle everything over the Internet. If you work smart – you never have to see any of the products or stock. Ideal for someone who has an eye for trends, market gaps and can grab opportunities when he/she sees them.

5. CHAT LINE

Some people just like to talk. Whether it's about the weather, politics or the latest gossip – they just want to talk! Are you a good listener? Then why not get your self one of those 0860 telephone lines where people pay and extra premium if they phone that number. These differ from country to country. Many competition hotlines use them, as well as mobile phone campaigns. Arrange with your local telephone company to have such a line connected to your phone. Now advertise in local newspapers, classified, free ads and on the Internet so that people can phone your number to talk about anything they want to. If they simply want a friendly voice to talk to, if they want a get something off their mind, if they need to share an experience, etc. Please note that unless you are a qualified practitioner, you cannot offer an advice service. You simply offer a chat/listening service. I dare you! You will be surprised at the amount of lonely people out there that just need someone to talk to!

6. CHILDREN'S LETTER SERVICE

In today's Internet driven world, this idea may seem old fashioned. BUT, that's exactly why it should cotton on today. Do you remember being a child and receiving a letter in the post? Wasn't that the best feeling ever? Children get excited when they receive something in the post. Are you good at keeping in touch and writing letters? If not, what about just sending a birthday card or greeting card on a special occasion? You can advertise in various family magazines and have the parents subscribe for 6 months to a whole year. Offer various packages and take into consideration rising postage costs! You could create standard letters in a handwriting font on the computer and print them in say blue ink so that they still look hand written. Then you simply fill in the name of the child. However, I would try and keep this personal and actually write the letters. You would be doing something unique. If you have a good handwriting; that's a bonus!

7. COMMUNITY PROJECT ORGANISER

With the decay of council and municipal services, coupled with greed and corruption in government, community services have began to suffer immensely. Do you care about others around you and the welfare of the community you live in? Are you good at organising events, bringing people together and basically managing community incentives and projects? This can all be done from the comfort of your own home, and at the same time change the community you live in and make life more positive around you. There is a big need for people who can make community projects happen. Check the state/provincial laws as to costs that can be deducted for administrative fees, and take your money from this. You may be surprised at just how high the legally allowed administrative costs for most of these 'non profit organisations' actually are. Ideally though, you should care for the community too; passion drives success!

8. COPYWRITER

You can do this job from anywhere, even the beach. All you need is a computer and an Internet connection. Of course you can even doing it from home manually and collect the necessary paperwork from companies in your area as well. You need to have a good grammatical knowledge of English (or language of the country you live in) and have a flare with words so that you can write in a convincing, persuasive and compelling manner so that companies approach you to write their copy for websites, adverts, sales brochures, press releases, Blog posts etc. You basically make what they want to sell sound awesome! If you can do this, here's a huge opportunity! Create a few examples of powerful copy and approach companies around you. Place an ad in the local paper that attracts companies to you. If you have the gift of writing great copy, your advert should do exactly that!

9. DATA ENTRY

For flexible hours and a steady income, one should give data entry some consideration. Many companies need data entered into forms, either manually or electronically. They pay per entry/form completed that means that you can go back and forth and complete the data as you have time in your day. This is especially convenient for mothers with babies where the normal routine can be constantly disrupted.

10. DATING AGENCY

Don't laugh! Some of the wealthiest people out there run dating agencies. Have a look at some of the up market glossy magazines and you will see full-page ads of exclusive agencies. We have billions of people on the earth today and not everyone is outgoing and makes friends easily. You could already be a good networker and have connected single friends together. Why not take it a step further and build up a small and exclusive agency that is initially area specific (i.e. where you live) and as you build up a name, you spread your reach. You have a basic registration fee with an interview and then you connect people together.

11. DIRTY TALK

The title says it all. If the idea offends you – there are 49 others! These ideas are general and tailored for many tastes. Do you have any idea how much money people make that talk dirty over the phone? This is a business that has been going on for ages. You just need to be broad-minded, have a good clear voice and not easily offended. You would have to cater to many weird tastes and fetishes, but if you are being paid per minute, it may be something to consider. Also, it's the easiest job to do in your pyjamas! You would need a special phone line where callers pay on a time basis; this you will have to investigate with your national phone company and set up a special line. You could even do this via SMS on your mobile phone! Most competitions work on a cost per SMS entry to make up funds.

12. ENTERTAINMENT AGENCY
Up and coming pop groups, singers, comedians, magicians and various other specialty acts could all benefit from your services. You must be well organised and have a good knowledge of events, clubs and other venues, as well as contacts in the corporate market for conferences. Naturally you will need a keen eye for talent. Contact your clients regularly, know your acts and who and what they are suitable for, and be good at marketing your services. Never book acts you haven't seen and make sure you only deal with reliable entertainers. Your commission should be around 15 - 25% of the artist's fee. If you want a niche market, limit yourself to a handful of entertainers that you can trust 100%. In that way you remain exclusive and give a top service to your client and the entertainers. You want to be able to place the right entertainer for the right function. With hundreds of names on your books this is not possible and you lose that personal touch. You can take the whole 'agency' concept further and include famous 'lookalike' people, celebrities, sports personalities and actors for stage and screen. The sky is the limit.

13. ESCORT AGENCIES
No, not a brothel! As soon as people hear the words escort agency, they associate it with some seedy dump in a run down area. Why don't you change that? Here is a reality check! Many single business people (male and female) are in your city on business trips and often need a partner to attend a business function with them. That's it, nothing else but a

person of similar intellect who will partner them for the event. Nothing else afterwards – just company! Set up an exclusive business agency that you market to companies who have regular events and functions. Be upfront and transparent and be clear in your advertising that your escorts are business people, keen on networking with other business people in similar fields. For a fee they will partner other business people to events. Naturally you screen everyone and connect people with similar interests. Plus, your agency consists of businessmen and women. I haven't seen many of these agencies around... could this be the next big business idea?

14. FREELANCE SALES AGENT

Sales does not always involve traveling and being on the road. Today much selling is done on the Internet and via emails. So in essence, it's a purely admin based job. More and more companies are willing to use freelance sales agents who work on a commission only. If you have the discipline and some clever IT techniques to make this happen – then it is a great work from home opportunity. You could also represent various companies to add variety to your range.

15. GRAPHIC DESIGNER

Yes, people go to college to study graphic design. However, you may be a natural and just good at drawing clever designs or cartoons. Basically if you can draw well, here is an opportunity. Many companies need good logos, or drawings for training manuals, adverts etc. Ideally you can scan everything into a computer and digitise what you draw. However, not everyone has all this technology. Hence even if you are drawing on a sketchpad you can even sell that picture to others around you. This is a job where you have to build up a brand and a name. However, remember, a picture says a thousand words! If you have the talent, this can be a great business to be in. You could even create your own 'clip art' collection and sell one off user rights per picture. The scope is endless.

16. HANDWRITING ANALYSIS

Some people may still scoff at Tarot cards and some of the other New Age services out there. However, handwriting analysis is a proven science. There are tons of books and course available on this and it is fairly easy to learn - plus really interesting too. This is a service you can offer without leaving the home. People can post, fax or email you handwriting samples and you can analyse them from the comfort of your own home. The scope is endless! You can approach recruitment firms, companies to do a character analysis, police to analyse criminal's handwriting, or even the general public as a niche service.

17. HOLIDAY HOME SWAPS

Organising holiday home swaps for a basic fee is a great home business. You start by connecting friends in different countries together and arranging for them to stay in each other's homes, thus saving money and having extra cash to pay you a 'finders fee.' As you get comfortable with this you can advertise in travel publications, Internet sites and offer a holiday home swap service. I would strongly suggest that you view each home and do detailed research on the homeowners so that you connect the right people. You do not want an up market couple from Beverly Hills doing a house swap with a couple from a housing estate in London – that's not going to work. Thus it is imperative to know your clients.

18. HOMEBUYERS INFORMATION SERVICE

This is something I have not come across before and could easily develop into a unique specialised service. When families want to buy a home in a new suburb or area, as well as companies – they do not always know what the area is like. If you have been living in your suburb for years, you no doubt know and understand the politics, culture, gossip, schools, shops and everything about your suburb. Are there environmental problems? What's the traffic like? Is it an up market area or have drugs become a problem in certain streets? These are all factors which are extremely important to people wanting to move to your area. Naturally this also changes over time so it is imperative to always be up to date as to what is happening around you. You can offer basic information for a set fee as well as more detailed reports for companies at a higher rate.

19. HOUSE SITTING

It's as the title says – you sit in someone else's house! Many people do not like to leave their house unattended when going on vacation, or on business trips. They would much rather prefer a reliable trusted person to live in their home while they are away - specially for security reasons. Yes many people follow the home swapping route with people in other countries, but most people do not. For a fee you can offer to house sit while someone is away. The coolest thing about this job is that you still have the time to do any of the other 49 home business idea in this booklet! You simply have a weekly rate that you charge and best of all is that the water and lights bills is for the owner of the house you are watching over, and not for you!

20. INTERNET RESEARCHER

Wikipedia and Google have changed the way we live. As a baby boomer I clearly remember sitting in a library for hours doing research on school projects and even business marketing when I was older. Today all that information is accessible from the comfort of your home and via the Internet. Many people doing research for studying, environmental planning, business plans, etc. do not have the time to do the required research. Thus you can offer an Internet research service where you will collect website addresses and/or information required by your client. As this can be quite time consuming, make sure you come to a clear agreement of payment terms. Either charge per hour of research, or for a specific amount of targeted information.

21. INSURANCE MIDDLE MAN

Although this book focuses on home admin related business ideas, you may well be an extremely good networker that just has a gift for connecting people. You may have a large social circle of friends, but you may also have a clever knack of sourcing contacts and connecting people via the Internet on the social media. Insurance brokers and advisors are constantly looking for contacts to approach with their products. Offer a service where you connect them with a specific target audience and ask a finder's fee, or even your own commission.

22. INVESTING

Many people have played the stock market and bought and sold shares as a hobby. A friend of mind recently retired and he has taken to investing on-line through a brokerage. He reads up daily what is happening in the world, informs himself of current events and invests accordingly. Impressively he started out with a small amount and as skills grew, his profits increased. Please note that this is a home business idea fro people who know and understand investing and who have the skills to do it themselves. You could be doing this right now as a hobby, but as is often the case, with the right further education and training it could become a great source of income, all from the comfort of your own home via your computer or mobile phone.

23. INVOICING SERVICE

As the modern world becomes more 'work from home' focused, handling invoicing for companies is becoming an increasingly popular service. You don't need any special training or skill. Most of the time companies will have their own template which you install on your computer and simply complete. Basically you offer to send out and follow up on all invoices for the finance department of companies. It's a specialised service, but one which many companies would like to outsource. Advertise your services to companies in your area. Or even approach companies far away who can send you everything via email.

24. KISSO-GRAM

There are many students looking to make an extra buck... not to mentioned older people too! What about interviewing outgoing candidates and building up a data base of people that are prepared to go out and deliver gifts, awards, invites etc. in character as a kiss-o-gram girl, stripper, hunk, nurse, witch, etc. Keep it 'above board' and market it to businesses & wealthy people who would make use of such a service. Keep a strict professional image and make sure your talent understands this as well. Simply take a commission on every call out.

25. MAGAZINE ARTICLES

Can you write stories? Are you could at researching topics of interest and writing about them? Every magazine published today needs contributors! Did you know that many actually pay for articles? Many of the mainstream magazines have competitions for contributions around certain themes and there are cash prizes if a readers letter is published. As an example, Readers Digest magazine pays for jokes they use. The print media has not gone out of fashion, if anything there are more magazines being printed today than ever before. All you need is to read through a few back copies to get an idea of what is required, and then start writing.   Many people make a handsome side income from this, plus become well known as their name starts appearing in magazines throughout the country. Once you become an established name, editors will start approaching you and you could even end up having a regular monthly column!

26. MAILING LIST BROKER

We all hate spam! The main reason is that the spam we get are mostly mass mailers and not pertinent to our needs and wants. So why not build up unique targeted mailing lists and offer to send out targeted mails for companies. There are many auto-responder companies out there that will handle your address lists for a reasonable monthly fee. Aweber is great for this! Search for companies that need to target their advertising to a certain group, and offer to do mail shots at a certain cost per mail, or package price. In the past letters where sent by snail mail and companies needed people to insert advertising into envelopes and deliver bulk mails to the post office. Although this is slowly fading away, the possibilities still exist. Think about it, when last have your received a nicely hand-written offer from a companies.

27. MAIL ORDER BUSINESS SUPPLYING ABSOLUTELY ANYTHING

This is a business ideally suited for someone who enjoys surfing the Internet and looking for bargains on the web. From health food, arts & crafts to antiques! Advertise a mail order business where you will source any product for clients at the best possible price. Requests come in and you search for various options on the Internet and offer these to your client. The client then chooses what he wants, pays you electronically and you then conclude the transaction and have the item posted to him directly.

28. MAIL ORDER FORWARDING AGENCY

Many companies would like a prime address in the city centre. Often one can rent a small office or even larger premises within the city centre at reasonable rates. One now offers outlying companies the facility of using your 'prime address' for delivery of their mail, parcels, etc for a monthly fee. Again, you will have to work out your pricing according to the amount of mail. You can include telephone answering services here as well, as many people tend to be 'dial code' conscious as well.

Ever seen the adverts in airline magazines for prime London office space? This is exactly what they are doing. Of course you then also have to come to an arrangement with the company as to when and how often they collect their mail, or whether you deliver it at a certain fee. Here you can do so personally, or bring in a courier company to do it for you to which you add a commission for the client's account.

29. MORTGAGE & LOAN ORIGINATOR

Excellent commissions can be made from helping people arrange loans and mortgages. Your main task will be taking phone enquiries, gathering information and filling in application forms. To get started you will need to contact a bank/loan firm that uses independent agents. You may need to pay for a license to operate as an agent, or go through some training. Once established, advertise in your local and regional newspapers and make contact with estate agents in your area.

30. PERSONAL MANAGER

This is very similar to running an entertainment agency, except that you limit yourself to one or two celebrities ONLY! Many well-known personalities are creative and want to focus on the art, rather than on admin. Also, many are extremely busy and don't have the time to do this. Thus if you can find a busy celebrity and offer to run their life for them; it's a win-win situation. You charge between 10-15% commission and you arrange everything. Book flights, hotels, card, and even find them bookings. I would focus on one only and maximum take on two at most.

31. PERSONALISED NUMBER PLATES

Had you mentioned personalised plates to someone a few years ago they would have laughed at you. Today it is big business in some countries. Basically you will need to buy new, source old number plates in the classifieds, at auctions or from car dealers. Now you have to find buyers for these personalised plates. Research the legalities and understand the costs involved in transferring ownership in your name. Hence you will need to work on a quick turnaround time, ideally where you don't have to take ownership and where you simply source number plates for people wanting a specific name. Various car magazines such as the Auto Trader are good to market your services. Today most of this can be done on the Internet and run from a home office.

32. PRINTING BROKER

The printing industry has become hugely competitive, especially with the digital printing presses available today. Furthermore, reliable printers are also much in demand. Once again, if you are a good networker and know a little about the industry, you can quickly build up a list of good reputable printers. Some will specialise in foil printed business cards while others will focus on 'Publishing On Demand Books.' Then again you get those printers that specialise in printing on weird objects in unique shapes and in small quantities. The sky is the limit. You merely act as middle man and advertise to promotional companies, ad agencies, pr companies and basically anyone that needs printing done, and you source the right printer and add your commission onto the print costs.

33. PROMOTIONS AND COMPETITION ORGANISER

Here is an industry which many people think is easy, hence it has become over saturated over the years. However, the recent recession sorted the good from the bad quite quickly. If you have good organisational skills, a fertile imagination and love people; this is a must! Yes, you have event's organisers that are always at the events, but if this is not for you, you can employ the right staff to be at the event. The crux of this job is that it needs something who is exceptional at bringing the right people together and that can come up with clever ideas that will draw people to promotions and competitions. From shopping malls to retail giants – everyone does promotions. It is a huge market and most businesses have a marketing budget.

34. PUBLIC EVENTS ORGANISER

Here's another industry that many people think is easy, hence many people have lost lots of money and also done much harm to the industry. This is suited to someone with exceptional organiSational skills and a person that can get a crowd together quickly. There are many up and coming entertainers and speakers out there that would love to fill a hall with an audience. If you have this skill you will always have work. Simply charge a fee per head/ticket sold and offer to fill venues or create a buzz that results in venues being sold out.

35. PROOFREADING

You need a good knowledge of grammar, preferably a formal education in the language you will proofread. Every author needs someone to proofread his/her novel for mistakes. Not just spelling, but grammatical mistakes too. A spell grammar check on a computer program does not identify all errors. We still need the human eye and mind to do this. Are you talented in this field? Have someone pay you to read and correct their work!

36. RECIPE E-BOOKS & EXCHANGE

Food and cooking programs are huge on television today. Suddenly celebrity chefs are bigger than actors and sports stars! Everyone eats and everyone loves good food. This is no longer something that only appeals to housewives! If you have a knack for cooking and are creative with food, create your own weekly recipes under different themes. Bring out a recipe newsletter - write a book. Have recipe competitions or swap recipes with others. Design and sell new themed recipe books every few months. The sky is the limit here.

37. REMINDER SERVICE

Another simple idea that requires minimal set-up and has huge potential. Professional people such as doctors and dentists employ full time secretaries to phone patients and remind them of their appointments. This takes up much time and costs many professional extra money. Why not offer a reminder service at a monthly fee to all the doctors, dentists and lawyers in your area? You could even add an extra fee and do follow-up appointments. Approach all doctors and dentists in your area and offer to do this service for them, for a set monthly fee. There will be other professionals who will require this service as well. Also consider advertising in industry related professional publications.

38. RENT OUT A ROOM/GARAGE

Many people don't realise that they actually have extra space in their homes. Often someone just needs to rent space to store items. An empty garage is ideal for this and you earn money for doing nothing. Many single people and especially students need a room to rent. Ideally it should have its own shower and toilet so that the person can be independent from your home. There is nothing worse than having a stranger in your home and use your bathroom. Thus is you have a spare self-contained outside room; this extra rental income adds wonderfully to covering the monthly home costs.

39. REVIEW SERVICE

Do you enjoy reading? This could be books, e-books or Blogs. Offer your review service to magazines and publications that have critics review written products and even films. You need to keep an open mind, be objective in your review approach and send it in. again, once you have built up a name for yourself, editors will start approaching you.

40. SECRETARIAL SERVICES AGENCY

You have two options here: source reliable secretaries and hire them out, taking a commission. Or offer a home secretary service where you take over certain secretarial admin related duties for a company at a specified monthly fee. Again you can approach companies in your area or place an ad in the classifieds in the press of on the Internet. Stick to basic services and make sure you have specific prices for specific amounts of work. You may be a specialist in Excel – and could hence offer specialised services in Excel only.

41. SPECIALIST SERVICES

Basically you would need to look at an avenue that you enjoy and have a keen interest in. Do some research to see if there are enough people in this field, and then offer to source products, information and services for them. Many hobbyists have started like this and within a few years have developed specialised businesses. Here are some areas of interest; artists and craft worker's, Astronomy, business directories, candle making supplies, comics & fantasy books, health foods & supplements, jewellery making products, ladies lingerie, magic tricks and jokes, microscopes & telescopes, party supplies, self improvement products, sports memorabilia, toy trains and accessories, etc. There are tons of specialised hobbies where people would require specific services and information.

42. SURPRISE GIFT PACKAGES

You could be one of those factory shop junkies and know where all bargains are to be had in your city. Why not try a 'Surprise Gift Package' service where you offer to put together and make up "Surprise Gifts' for all occasions. From children's parties, anniversaries, and stag nights to 50th birthdays – you simply put together a real nice value for money package. You can further diversify into offering fun packages to themed packages. The sky is the limit. Also consider having a range in prices so that you cater to all markets.

43. TELEPHONE ANSWERING SERVICE

Many companies do not want a computer generated answer service or recorded message when they are out of the office. They prefer a real live person answering the phone. It may be a small company with limited call per day, i.e. one-man enterprise, or it may be a larger company scaling down. You can have various phone lines coming into you home and allocate certain numbers to certain companies, or you can answer the phone in a generic manner and then ascertain whom the caller is looking for, and take the appropriate message. Using a blue tooth headset you can go about your daily household chores, gardening, etc. and still answer all the calls! I wouldn't charge a 'per call rate' as this would mean that you have to be on 'standby' for someone that may only get one call per week! Thus you should have a minimum monthly rate that increases depending on the average number of expected calls per month.

44. TRANSLATION SERVICE

Do you speak two or three languages? There is a huge demand for people to translate documents into English or from English into another language. If you have Spanish, Chinese, French, German, etc skills it is a matter of approaching the various Consulate Generals and professional companies such as legal firms, tax consultants, training companies and offer the translation service at a per word/per page fee. Simultaneous translations at live seminars is also a market!

45. TRANSCRIPTIONIST

Huh? Ever watch a court drama and seen that person punching away on a small weird looking machine? They are taking notes/keeping record of the court proceedings. These need to be typed up into full transcripts. Ever watched a training/educational video on the Internet and received a free e-book of the video? There is no software that transcribes video into the written word as yet. People are needed to type out this information. Medical transcriptions are very much in demand today where you transcribe medical reports dictated by doctors. Visit my site, www.wolfgangriebe.com and subscribe to my free video course on Life Skills. Every fortnight you will receive a free E-book on what you watched the previous week. Someone had to type out that video course. It was me! If I knew of someone to do this for me, I would have jumped at the opportunity. Over and above the legal sector, there are literally thousands of speakers, educators and trainers with video products on the Internet that want these transcribed.

46. TRAVEL ADVICE SERVICE

I have worked in over 144 countries in my career. Today I speak about Customer Service in the travel and hospitality industry. Why? I have the experience! Have you traveled a lot? Do you have experience in a certain field in tourism? Why not share it with others? The tourist industry is one of the largest in the world. Some cities have millions of tourists per year. Why not offer an advice service for people who want to travel. If you have a specialised area, offer them a comprehensive advice booklet at a fee, or even offer to answer specific questions at a fee per question rate. Providing the right objective advice for tourists can save people thousands and prevent them being ripped off. Word of mouth from satisfied tourists can make your business grow very quickly.

47. TYPING SERVICE

This would include the typing of novels from hand written notes and manuscripts. Typing letters and memos for business professionals recorded on a Dictaphone/DAT machine etc. Doing transcription for court cases and medical cases. If you have typing skills this is something that can be done from home and emailed back to the clients.

48. VIRTUAL ASSISTANT

This job didn't exist a few years ago! Seems India is leading the stakes in virtual assistants at present. Basically anyone can provide administrative, secretarial and clerical support to anyone anywhere in the world today. I would start by offering this service to businesses in my area and build it up from there. Think about it... the person contracting you to do these limited services is saving on full time employment costs as well as office space. Most of the time people requiring these services only need an hour or two worth of work at most per day. This enables you to build up a good selection of clients with various needs. Hence the variety of the work keeps it interesting too. Simply advertise your services initially to companies in your vicinity.

49. WRITE, SELF-PUBLISH AND SELL HOW TO GUIDES

What is an expert? People say it is someone who researches information and then puts together a summary of everything he/she has researched. With the Internet today, practically anything can be researched. Find some popular topics or issues and spend a few days researching the subject. Then compile a simple guide (such as this range of E-Books) and offer them to the market out there. This is particularly fun if you tackle a topic which you enjoy. Many people have later gone to talk about their specialty topics and used these speeches as another source of income. Remember that when you write something, you are an author... and authority is just an extension of the word author. People like paying for the services of an authority! Alternatively, a guide to growing outdoor plants or vegetables should also prove popular. If you would rather sell existing titles on these subjects, then see what's available and find a reliable source of supply. Best would be to research the subject and write and publish your own guides. Compile a catalogue and advertise in the classified ads of gardening magazines.

50. WRITING SKILLS

This could be a booklet on it's own! Are you creative and enjoy writing? Then you have a huge range of opportunities available to you. These ideas have just increased the total ideas in this booklet! You could: Launch and edit various E-zines on the internet; Write books, fiction or non-fiction, from crime stories to crossword puzzle books; Write greeting card verses for card producers; Become a ghost writer for wannabe authors; Create a newsletter on a niche subject; Jokes, letters and short stories to magazines; Produce a directory, whether business or niche market; Write a biography on someone famous. The possibilities are endless!

YOUR OWN ADMINISTRATIVE HOME BUSINESS IDEAS

IDEAS WITH ARTS & CRAFTS

50 Home Business Ideas with Arts & Crafts! Yes here are 50 ideas covering a wide range of fields and topics. They are mainly ideas that you can run from your home. In other words, ideas that involve a spare room, converted garage or extra space somewhere in the home, and that you could in essence also do in your pyjamas!

1. APRONS IN VARIOUS STYLES

Aprons make great gifts as well as novelty gifts if you come up with unique designs and funny sayings. Also, restaurants and restaurant chains may well have need for tailor-made aprons. You need a pattern, a sewing machine and some clever ideas. It's something you don't see a lot of today, so if you can come it at a good price with a unique design, I see no reason why this should not be a good market.

2. CANDLE MAKING

Candle making has been around for years. I remember as a child my mom making candles in old yogurt cups. Today the this craft has become so much more advanced and candle designs have become works of art. Whereas in the olden days we had candles for blackouts; today it's more for creating a nice mood. Even scented candles are hugely popular. Once again, using your imagination you can become very creative, from adding dry leaves to glitter into the process. The sky is the limit here. Go price decent table candles in your local supermarket and you will be shocked at how expensive they have become. Hence if you can make them at a competitive price and come up with your own unique brand; there is a potential market. Initial outlay will be minimal and there is enough information freely available on the

Internet to teach you everything you need to know about candle making.

3. CAR SEAT COVERS AND CAR BOOT LINERS

Every car is different, so I would target a limited number of models and brands to start with. In fact I suggest you do a market research of the 5 or 6 most popular brands of vehicles in your area, and then you design seat covers and boot liners for these models only. You will need an industrial overlocker to finish off the covers and liners, plus a reliable supplier. As many supermarkets sell cheap car seat covers, I would recommend starting off with the boot liners and building a name through this.

As soon as people realise that your name stands for quality and uniqueness, they will be more apt to spent more money on a quality made seat cover. Remember, most people have at least one car. I often collect stuff from the nursery or hardware store and end up putting a blanket in my boot. A custom made boot liner is definitely something I would consider buying and am sure that most other people would too.

4. CAT TREES

Recently I bought a small kitten and if you know cats, they scratch on everything. Hence I looked for one of these cat trees/towers. I was stunned at the prices! With off-cut wood and off-cut carpet I could make the same thing for next to nothing. Just do a search on Google and look at the hundreds of pictures and designs. Approach a lumber store and ask for their off-cuts. Do the same with a carpet company. Go ahead and start building cat tree. With a bit of creativity and keeping in mind that cats enjoy sitting high up and looking down on the world around them; you can start a booming business.

5. CHESS SETS AND SMALL ORNAMENTS

Having travelled throughout the world in my career I have seen chess sets in most countries and cities on this globe. Each representing various cultures and designs that include every conceivable type of figurine – often making it difficult to recognise which piece represents a pawn or a bishop. Once again, creativity plays a role. Can you design a chess set that is different and where the pieces can be recognised, yet still are unique? If you can – there is a good possibility you can supply the local chess club, schools, collectors, gift shops and even mail order off the Internet.

6. CHILDREN'S SOFT TOYS & STUFFED ANIMALS

Every couple I know that has children, have a box or drawer with scrap off-cuts of material. Most families I know have a sewing machine. Put these two together and start making small stuffed animals, teddy bears, etc. Again patterns can be found in magazines and on the Internet. Ask your friends to clear out all their drawers and give you all their scrap material. Hence start up production should be minimal and once you start selling your first creations, you start using that money for different materials and build up your business.

7. COLOURFUL QUILTS FOR CHILDREN

The sky is the limit! You can use that same sewing machine, or do this by hand in front of the TV. Again, off-cuts can be used to create a colourful quilt. You can add designs, figurines and anything you can think of. Like all other crafts; once people see what you have the word will spread. Also use all mediums to market your quilts.

8. COMFY BEDS FOR PETS

The money people spend on pets is unbelievable! Just walk into your veterinary clinic or local pet shop and see the stuff available for dogs and cats, especially baskets and beds! If you can come up with a clever pillow design or comply quilt/blanket for pets and a cheaper price; you have a huge market. Once again I would start with scrap material around the house and even do patchwork style pillows for dogs. Once you have sold a few and made some money, you can go into specific designs.

9. COSTUME JEWELLERY

I am friends with many jewellers and costume jewellery has increasingly become popular over the years. If I look at what people are stringing together and selling as jewellery today, I don't think you need much talent to make money from this. You have bean shops in most major shopping malls where you get get the basic beads, clasps, etc. Now it's a case of being creative and coming up with some catchy designs. Start selling to your friend and social circle and eventually build it up to gift stores and the Internet.

10. CROSS STITCH PICTURES MARQUETRY PICTURES

If you have needle-craft skills and enjoy sewing, then this is something to consider. You can get simple ready-made starter kits from craft and sewing shops. Once you feel confident enough to develop your own designs you can sell them at craft fairs, through the Internet and to friends.

11. DENIM ACCESSORIES

Who doesn't own a pair of jeans today? If you are nifty on a sewing machine, consider making accessories that go with the jeans, such as handbags, hats, waistcoats and even shopping bags; all made from denim! Market them to various shops, Internet and to friends initially. The word can spread very quickly and your business could be in full blossom within a few weeks.

12. DESIGN A NEW BOARD GAME

Are you a specialist in a certain field? Why not design a fun board game around that product or industry. A friend of mine who enjoys network marketing just design a brilliant game explaining and teaching the whole MLM business. I see him making a fortune. Yes, it will take a lot of research and fine tuning, but the possibilities are endless. Either license it to an established game manufacturer, or launch it yourself.

13. DESIGNING, MAKING & SELLING BATH ROBES

Be honest, when have you not been tempted to take the bathrobe home from the hotel? A bathrobe is something special and great to keep you warm and comfortable after a bath. It is particularly suited to ladies who still want to put on make-up, do their hair, yet be warm and comfortable at the same time. Playing with different colours and motifs can result in an exclusive brand that you can market to clothing stores and shops specialising in nightwear.

14. DOLL MAKING

Dolls and earn you good money! But what about all the accessories such as the dresses, handbags, etc.? What about restoring old dolls and launching a 'Doll Hospital, or Clinic?Believe it or not, it's not just young girls that collect dolls, many adults do too. Many even keep their childhood dolls as a 'memento' of their youth. These dolls are mostly in need of repair as well. Couple your creative sewing skills with practical repairing skills and you can have a booming business.

15. DRAW CARTOONS

Here is a tough market to get into, but with determination, it can be a good sideline income. Can you draw? Are you quick witted? Few people are both. Nevertheless, if you pick up on news stories and can see the funny side of life, plus can draw cartoons; why not start your own cartoon character for magazines and other publications? Alternatively you may either just be witty, or just be a good artist. If you can't draw, but have the funny ideas, approach an editor and offer them a good dozen or so funny quips. If they like them they should give you 50% of the going rate and have their cartoonists do the final pick. Alternatively if you can do both, you can also start your own blog or webpage and sell your creations on-line.

16. FANCY DOG COLLARS AND COATS

I have a mini zoo at my home. We love animals. The other day I wanted to buy a new collar for my cat and was amazed at the selection and the prices. I genuinely thought to myself that I can make the same collars for a tenth of the price and asked at the Vet or pet shop; hence this idea. With a bit of creativity, a variety of nice materials I am convinced you can make this kinds of collars (for dogs and cats) at a huge mark-up and still come in cheaper the what is currently available.

17. FANCY DRESS ANIMAL COSTUMES

How many stores do you know that hire out fancy dress costumes? Maybe an old theatre has some stock, but for the most one needs to buy costumes at a joke shop and these are all mass made, resulting in a bad fit. If you can work with a sewing machine, it is easy to make various costumes, for adult and children. I know a lady living in the suburbs that started this – within a year she had added a new garage and now has a huge sample of outfits and is earning a huge steady sideline income.

Work out what the cleaning/dry cleaning costs are as well as the actual cost of making the outfit. Always ask for a deposit that covers the cost of making the item, (should they ruin the costume) and then charge a hire rate that is about 20% lower than buying the costume. It should work out that within 2 to 3 hires, you have recouped the costs 100%. After that it's all pure profit!

18. FLUFFY ANIMAL AIR FRESHENERS FOR CARS

Here comes another great idea using scrap material, Design and sew together animal shapes into which you can insert an air freshener. Find a fancy rubber cord so they can hang it from the rear view mirror, or even the rubber suckers so that they can stick it onto their car window. Alternatively just make animals that lie around the car and smell good!

19. FRAME AND SELL OLD PRINTS FROM BOOKS

Have you ever wanted to know what to do with all your old magazines and books? Here is the answer! Cut out unique pictures and photos and find attractive frames to put them into. You can even group photos together and have theme frames. The sky is the limit and all you need to do is purchase some frames from and art store. Many larger wholesale stores sell packs of 3 to 5 frames and one can use these to create sets of pictures. The sky is the limit.

20. FRAMED DECOUPAGE PICTURES

My mom used to be an artist and a clearly remember her creating a very good additional income by making decoupage pictures. In fact she even offered courses in decoupage. You can even order basic kits from a craft shop or through mail order and learn it yourself. Once again use your old books and magazines as a resource for pictures which you magical transform into decoupage pieces of art.

21. FUNNY CARICATURES

This is something I see very rarely. Do you have an eye for faces and characters? Can you quickly draw a person and include striking features? Can you do this in a humorous way? If yes, you don't have to busk on the side of the street or sit at craft markets waiting for passing traffic. You can approach companies and offer this service at events and conferences. Offer to to a caricature of each speaker on a day program at a conference. You can charge really good fees for this and it is a novel concept for companies.

22. HANGING BASKETS

A basket or box with 3 or 4 ropes connecting to a hook up top that can be hung from ceilings, roofs, tree branches etc. Quite simple to make and not only need contain flowers, but anything gimmicky! Word of mount, craft markets and the Internet allow opportunities for selling these.

23. GARDEN GNOMES & ORNAMENTS

I have seen gardens with whole families of gnomes – it's almost a tourist attraction! You can use your imagination here, from hand carved wooden gnomes to cast moulds of gnomes that are painted in bright colours. As with all crafts, your imagination is the only thing that limits you. These can also be offered to garden centres and nurseries, as well as sold at craft markets and on the Internet.

24. GIANT SOFT TOYS

Giant teddy bears and cuddle toys are a speciality gift and always popular to display at toy stores and generate sales. You can even create your own teddy characters. Proficiency at sewing and stitching is a must, and this can become a lucrative business.

25. GLASS SCULPTURES AND ORNAMENTS

I have seen glass blowers in Ireland and Russia, very little elsewhere. This is a dying art it seems. I am sure you can find someone in your country and hopefully (because of the niche market) they can teach you the art and you can design unique glass ornaments that can be sold for very good prices. Because of the exclusivity of this art, you can sell the ornaments at most places and a classy website would definitely help as well.

26. GLASS PAINTING

I know a glass painter who supplied a whole restaurant franchise nationally with his lamp designs. Well-painted glass panels, not just as wall hangings, but also as lamp shades, display ornaments, etc can be very different and stand out from the norm. If you are artistic, most art shops have glass paints and it's a fairly inexpensive hobby that can easily turn into a booming business.

27. HAND CARVINGS

In Africa wood carving can be found everywhere, but not so much in the rest of the world. It's a relaxing craft and if you have a talent for carving, it can be most fulfilling. From carving small to big items, from bowls to animals. From display unit ornaments to garden figures. The possibilities are endless. I have seen carvers do simply home bar notices where the writing is carved out of an odd shaped plank. These seemed to be very popular. Again, only your imagination limits you.

28. HAND PUPPETS FOR CHILDREN

I remember as a child having my own puppet theatre and watching puppet shows at the local library. My birthday parties always alternated between a magician and a puppet show. In my days it was simply hand puppets with a head and two arms controlled by one hand that fitted inside the puppet. If you are nifty on a sewing machine – these are really easy to make. If you are more adventurous and can tackle the Sesame Street style puppets – there is another huge market for you.

29. HOUSE NAMES AND NUMBERS

Here's something I would buy immediately, and the price would not be such an issue either. House names are unique. I struggled to find letter to put on the wall for my home. Most hardware stores only have numbers. This could be a huge market and you can design names and numbers from anything. I believe this can be a most fun, creative and also very lucrative business to start.

30. KITES

Kites have become increasingly popular again today. The designs have become incredible high tech and colourful. I still remember making rectangular kites from bamboo and brown paper and using a flour water mix as the glue. Family values and activities are starting to become important again. Making kites for father and son is a good angle. Even a bigger and a smaller kite as a pair. A search on the Internet will make your mouth water as to the possibilities.

31. KNITWEAR FOR BABIES AND YOUNG CHILDREN

I would be surprised if most readers look at this idea. Knitwear to most people is old fashioned! Think again! It is so in and so very popular. My sister in law started a business on the side and within a year had built a whole studio onto the house with 5 computerised machines. Today she has a booming business! Make no mistake, it's a lot of work, but with good quality and fair prices; there is a definite market. Research different trends and target a specific group so that you have your own niche, be it adults, children, babies or even school jerseys.

32. LEATHER CRAFTING

Many useful and practical items can be made with leather crafting; from belts, wallets, key rings, handbags to shoes. Just take a belt bought in a normal store, it never lasts more than a few months. Hand make your own from leather and sell this in the business sector! You can learn the basics from books or even YouTube videos. If you are creative; this is definitely an idea to consider.

33. LEG WARMERS, SCARVES/WOOLLEN HATS FOR CHILDREN

The title says it all. You can hand-make these initially and then as money comes in, buy machines to do this. Be colourful and use eye catching designs. Offer your products to boutiques and specialist stores in your area and let your reputation build up from there.

34. LOOSE CUSHION/ARM REST COVERS FOR LOUNGE SUITES

Furniture has become really pricy these day. How about offering arm rest covers and cushions that compliment an old lounge suite and bring it back to life again. For many people this is the only affordable practical option sprucing up their living rooms. A while back I had someone quote me and re-upholstering an old lounge suite – it was shocked. For a little bit more money I could have bought a brand new one. Hence I went the cushion and arm rest option as well.

35. LUCKY CHARM KEY RINGS AND BRACELETS

Yes even in the 21st century, people are still superstitious and lucky charms are as popular as ever before. A lucky horseshoe, rabbit's foot, or four-leaf clover made in a plastic, silver, gold or enamelled design still sells today! Whether on bracelets, pendants for necklaces or keyring attachments, the sky is the limit. Offer them to souvenir shops in tourist areas as well as marketing them on the Internet.

36. MATERNITY WEAR FOR EXPECTANT MOTHERS

Walk through any shopping mall in Europe and the UK... all you see is expectant mothers and mothers with babies. The maternity market is HUGE. Also it's not so popular amongst fashion designers, so there is way less competition. If you can come up with a design that emphasises the woman's femininity, instead of her size, you will have a money spinner. Women talk to each other and word of mouth marketing can spread your designs like wild fire. If you can make dresses; this is a serious option to consider. Put your designs on the Internet and allow the ladies to order by mail as well.

37. MIRRORS

Like most other topics, designs are limited by your imagination. Whether you frame the mirrors, paint on them, stick sea shells around them – the possibilities are endless. You can even offer to install mirrors in peoples homes to enlarge a room or add depth and atmosphere to certain areas in a home. Find a supplier and arrange a good price on mirrors. You can even use off-cuts in different sizes and shapes and make a unique 'modern' pieces.

38. MOSAIC PICTURE KITS

As a child in the 70's I remember my mom making designs with mosaic. It was popular to have dolphins and mermaids mosaic designs in the floor of swimming pools in the 70's and 80's. One doesn't really see that anymore. Today it something new and fresh again; that's how old it is. It's easy to learn and many courses are available from books and on the Internet. Come up with some unique designs that can be added to table tops, on walls, or even as part of bathroom and kitchen tiles to enhance current designs. Have a few designs on display at hardware and specialist stores to market your services.

39. NOVELTY CAPS

The world is cap crazy. Everyone has them and companies will buy in bulk for company events. Caps designed around sports themes are hugely popular. I saw a cap that can hold a can of beer/cold drink with a straw that runs down the side; it makes drinking easier. In fact I recently saw a cap that can hold a can on either side of the head, almost like Micky Mouse ears. Most people at this event bought one! Once again, the fertility of your imagination will be the deciding factor in how much money you can earn from your caps.

40. NOVELTY CANDLE HOLDERS

Whether wood, metal, resin or anything else you can think of, unique candle holders always stand out. A plain white candle can look so different in the right holder. From 'one-off' designs to sets of holders. From modern funky designs, to animal holders to tubes, From standing holders to hanging holders. The sky is the limit.

41. NOVELTY CLOCKS

You can buy clock mechanisms for cheap. In fact many craft stores have them in over supply. Recently I saw a whole lot of old 33 vinyl records converted into clocks. They already had the hole in the middle. You can even stick novel pictures on the records or spray/paint them different colours. In fact you can use any flat item and even frame it. As always, it all depends on your creativity. Come up with something funky and new, and people will buy it.

42. NOVELTY PAPERWEIGHTS

Years ago a friend of mine picked up riverbed rocks, stuck those 'moving' eyes on them and sold them as pet rocks and paper weight. He made a fortune at craft markets! Whether you want to cast designs from resin or plaster, or use available items and add a design to them, the possibilities are endless. The more shiny and high tech, the more suited to an office environment.

43. OVEN GLOVES AND IRONING BOARD COVERS

Every house needs oven gloves and everybody irons clothes! That alone is an indication of how huge this market is. When last, or have you ever seen funky oven gloves and ironing board covers. If you are creative and have a few sample pattern and the basic S,M,L glove sizes, here is an opportunity to not only supply novel designs to your neighbourhood, but to bigger retail stores as well.

44. PERSONALISED ELECTRIC PLUG COVERS

The majority of homes have white plug and light covers. Occasionally one may find a metal or other color finish. What about hand painting them with unique designs and colours or sticking on unique pictures or finishes? Yes, big home stores are staring to stock a larger variety of covers, but the market is huge. You can personalise light and plug covers for shops, companies as well as private homes. You creativity will determine your success.

45. PERSONALISED MUGS

I remember my mom used to paint on porcelain and make exquisite dinner sets. She would buy the plain white crockery from a good supplier and paint the design onto it. You can simplify this process by approaching pottery companies to make your own brand of cups for you, or you can make them yourself. Even a good supplier of basic white mugs allows you to paint on them or even add beads to the handles. The sky is the limit. Be creative and approach restaurants, pubs and companies and offer to make personalised mugs for them.

46. REPRODUCE OLD PRINTS USING GLAZING AND CRACKING TECHNIQUES

Any modern print can be made to look old by giving it a yellow stained effect, and glazing it with special varnish which gives it a crackled look. Add a suitable antique frame and you have an authentic looking old master. Crackle varnish can be bought at most arts and craft stores. You merely take any picture and put it through this process. Easy to sell and easy to make.

47. SKETCH STYLISH INK DRAWINGS OF PRIVATE RESIDENCES

If you can draw, this is a great idea for upmarket areas, as these people like 'showing off' their house and possessions. Once one person has this, they will all want the same for their home. Offer the pictures in different sizes and frames and personalise everything to fit in with the home concerned. Even if you can't draw, you can take photos and create a sketch effect in PhotoShop. Add a few more creative ideas and you still have a novel drawing for this market.

48. UNUSUAL BOOKENDS

Here the possibilities are endless. Think of ideas that appeal to a large group of people, such as movie fans or sport fans. Your design could be based on a pair of movie cameras, or an icon from a famous movie, or even a super hero. The bookends could be made to match or be completely different, as long as they work as a pair. You can pick up items at garage sales and flea markets and let your creative flair do the rest!

49. VARIOUS UNUSUAL SCULPTURES

The sky is the limit! Whether you take apart an old computer and stick the components together with parts from an old washing machine – there are no rules. You can create the wackiest, zaniest sculptures from junk, and sell then for big bucks! Nothing is stopping you from adding wood, stone or even resin to the whole thing. The more creative you are, the better. For all you know, someone may offer to display your collection in an art gallery! This is fun and a way of using up all the old junk in the home, and creating money with it.

50. WATERPROOF CUSHIONS FOR GARDEN FURNITURE

This service you can advertise in home and garden magazines to start with. Many people purchase garden furniture without cushions, and others have old furniture with weathered cushions. I recall my mom always took the cushions indie when we were not using the garden furniture. Hence imagine you can offer waterproof cushions? You could even make replacement covers as well.

Dear Optimist, Pessimist, and Realist,

While you guys were busy arguing about the glass of water, I drank it!

Sincerely, The Opportunist

— — — — —

Life is 10% what happens to you and 90% how you react to it.

YOUR OWN ARTS & CRAFTS HOME BUSINESS IDEAS

IDEAS IN DESIGN & PRINT

There are a number of bigger jobs that require no capital upfront where the customer to give you a 50% deposit before starting the job. You use the money to purchase everything you need and the rest is pure profit. The design & print industry is a great opportunity to really offer specialised services that can bring in excellent incomes on the side and easily become a full time job. Many people already have a computer & printer, so many of these ideas can be started right away!

1. 3D MAPS & INFORMATION GRAPHICS

Do a Google search on 3d Maps and Tourist Maps and you will understand what this is about. For many people a normal map is difficult to read. If you can create a simple almost 3D style map out of a complex city centre grid, or any other area, people will understand it better. Los Angeles tourist association has created a wonderful LA map with all the highlights and attractions. Even Dubai has one, but I have rarely seen this in other cities and especially not in small towns and villages. Here is a nice market. Even resorts could benefit from such a map. In fact any information pamphlet or map simplified with bigger print, less cluttered information and pictures improves the understanding of it. With research, the right creative thinking and good software you should be able to create stunning maps.

2. 3D PRINTING

Although 3D printing is still relatively new in 2013, it may very soon be available as readily as any normal printer. So, while it is still novel, the investment of such a printer is quite high, but the return on investment by being able to print literally any small item is huge. People may be looking for a part for a toy, a specific stature for the living room, a trinket from another country, etc. As I understand it, you can print form a picture too! Thus offering people a cost effective solution to find all sorts of objects which normally are difficult to source – you could be on a very good wicket with your 3D printing.

3. ADVERTS

Ad agencies, communication companies and PR people create adverts. If you have a creative flair and are good at designing, what is stopping you from creating eye catching and different ads. First approach smaller companies and charge lower rates. Build up a portfolio and then approach bigger companies with the aim of landing their whole ad campaign.

4. BOOK MARKERS FOR SOUVENIR SHOPS

Yes, iPads, Kindle and various other electronic readers are becoming increasingly popular. However, there is still a huge portion of the population that prefers a physical book in their hands. Hence this idea still has merit today! I can't think of one city today that doesn't have souvenir shops. Do some research and visit various stores in your area and see what they have to offer in terms of Bookmarks. Find a pretty touristy area in your city, take a photo and now create a fancy design incorporating this picture on a bookmark. Print them, laminate them and cut them to size with a guillotine and sell them to the souvenir stores. Don't limit yourself to one style. You could create a set of bookmarks, i.e. the Big 5 animals of Africa, or star signs that each have a unique picture of your city that relates to the meaning of the sign. Just use your imagination and be different.

5. BOOK PUBLISHING

POD (Publishing on Demand) printing has changed the entire publishing industry. Simply do a search on POD printers in your area and you will find a large selection of companies that can print from one to a thousand books at a moments notice. No longer to you have to take out a mortgage to print your own book. In fact www.amazon.com has https://kdp.amazon.com/en_US that is the self publishing POD side of amazon and you can set up your own book and order from as little as one copy from amazon of your own book.

This opens up a completely new field of business opportunities. If you have good DTP software such as Microsoft office, you can design and lay out your whole book, save it to PDF and have it printed. You can now write your own book, or collect poems, jokes, speeches from others and print a compilation book. Basically you can print books on any subject. Make sure you have permission to use the content, or write it yourself. Now market it correctly and away you go!

6. BOOK COVERS

This is a specialist field on its own. You would need to create your own templates for various sizes of books and/or understand how to work out the sizing of the spine of the book as this also needs a title and author name. You need a creative flair to be able to come up with catchy and novel covers that draw a potential reader to the book. A good cover can make a huge difference on sales. Your focus should be on simple, yet eye catching designs. Do some research and see what best selling covers look like. Speak to people in the industry and find out as much as you can.

Book publishing is so much more accessible to people today, hence many more books are written than ever before. It is a growing market and you can initially search for specialist associations whose members are more prone to write books, i.e. speaker associations, academia and colleges. Also bear in mind that there is a big shift towards E-books. These cover would require a slightly different design approach than your physical books.

7. CALENDARS

Every year I add a desk calendar in my office, another on the wall, as well as a small magnetic one on the fridge. These are always calendars I get for free from various companies. Approach any company that has their own calendar every year, and offer to design it for them. You can even approach printing firms that do this and show them a selection of your own designs with the hope that they may buy some and sell them. Approach companies that don't have calendars and offer them various designs. Make an arrangement with a printing company so that they offer you a special rate if you bring them orders. You can also offer these to souvenir, gift and stationary stores.

8. CARTRIDGE REFILL SERVICE

Have you noticed that most printers are cheaper than buying a full set of cartridges for the same printer? I have a mate who started a printer cartridge refill service. He now has a franchise of stores and is doing really well for himself. He basically started the business in his garage. Printer companies make a fortune and most of their profits from the cartridges. To learn how to refill one is simple. The only challenge is re-setting the chips on the cartridge. But once you have the gadgets to do this, it becomes a simple procedure. When you look at the real cost of buying ink in bulk, you can still sell the reconditioned cartridge at half the price of a new one and make huge profits.

9. CERTIFICATES

Decent software plus a creative flair and you are ready to design certificates for companies, schools, clubs, training centres and associations. Create a few examples and approach this wide range of sectors. The majority of stationary stores (including supermarkets) sell a selection of pre-packed marble style paper. Print your certificates and have them laminated. Alternatively small laminators can be bought inexpensively and are ideal for this job. Promote what you do directly to the various sectors/companies as well as office and stationary supply stores. You can even create a webpage with your designs. This is a very low cost start-up and relies mainly on your creative flair.

10. CD LABEL PRINTING

Although CD's and DVD's are slowly being replaced by digital media on hard drives, Blue Ray disks and disks for storage will still be around for many years. Most printers have their own built in CD label printing software. Once again programs such as PhotoShop are ideal and many templates are available for free on the Internet. A printer that prints on printable disks is fairly cheap, your printer may even have that facility already. Offer a small run printing service where you have designed the label. If the client wants large quantities, approach a large disc duplication company to do the job and add your profit onto their price.

11. CHILDREN'S BOOKS/POSTERS & EDUCATIONAL LEAFLETS

With POD printing, publishing your own kid's books is easy. Create a colourful story using big print and pictures. You can create educational messages on posters and in leaflets, marketing these to schools and kindergartens. The children's market is huge and most of them are sitting on tablets today, hence creating digital material is perfectly

12. CREATE BANNERS & POSTERS FOR PERSONALITIES

There are many 'personalities' who are not 'A' class celebrities, yet these are people in the public spotlight. Examples include professional speakers, politicians and entertainers. These people are ALWAYS on the lookout for clever designs around their marketing. They don't have budgets to pay ad agencies, but they have enough to make it worth your while. Because they are eager for exposure, their contact details are usually very easy to find. Approach them with a few examples of what you do and offer to design their pull out banners, posters, flyers and even business cards for them. In many instances they may require small quantities for specific events. If you can build a relationship with a handful of these personalities that work on a regular basis, they good provide and excellent additional income.

13. CREATE E-BOOKS

You don't even need to be a writer! Find a topic you are passionate about and do some research. Read up everything you can find on the subject and now write about it in your own words. Never copy and paste other people's writings! That's plagiarism! They say that when you copy one person's work, it's plagiarism, but when you read up on many people's work and combine this information into your own words, that's research! Pretty much the way this books has been put together! Now lay it out, add hyperlinks and create a nice PDF version of the book and sell it online! Build up a good stock of books as time goes by.

Also, don't be afraid to bring out free e-book that are 'teasers' or shorter versions of the main book. You could have a book with 100 tips to lose weight. Now bring out a mini version called 5 effective weight loos tips. At the end of this book advertise the main book. Market this book on your website and all your social media contacts. Blog about it everywhere and upload the book on free e-book sites for other to download. Everyone likes free stuff and if you have written a quality book with good take-home value, people will react to your advert at the end. Sometimes you have to give in order to receive. This is the exact method I initially used and still use today to market my books.

14. CREATE INSPIRATIONAL POSTERS

As an inspirational speaker, I know that this works. Many of my colleagues do this and it brings in a good constant income. Certain quotations are copyright free and one can freely use them. They have to be over a certain age and the law may differ in your country. So please check this out. You can either buy stock photos from a photo library, or take your own pictures. Source the right inspirational quotation and add this to the photo. Add a nice frame and sell these inspirational posters as downloads.

Of course you can print them, frame them and sell them to companies as well, either in sets or individually. You just need to make sure that the quotation and the picture work well together and appeals to the eye. Do a search and see what these kinds posters sell for! You could even bring out smaller sets in frames of market this to gift shops.

15. CREATE PRINTS

Yes, this is similar to the inspirational posters, but it is more specialised. There are many hobbyists and specialist markets out there. Why not source classic car pics, old buildings, or pics of animals, from house pets to penguins. Again you need to make sure that you are not infringing copyright. You can now load these pics into various DTP software, e.g. PhotoShop and add filters so that the pictures look old, sparkly, whatever. Create sets of these and sell them to the special interest groups in these sets. It would be to your advantage to find rare and unique pictures in each niche market that would be an attraction to buy. The range and market is pretty huge.

16. DESIGN SERVICE

Do you have an artistic flair? Are you good at creating designs on Photoshop or any similar programs? If yes, why not consider offering to design layouts for business cards, leaflets, adverts and newsletters. The client approached you with an idea and you put it into pictures/fancy design. You need basic computer software, and eye for detail coupled with a creative flair and you can charge a service for doing what comes naturally! With more advanced software you can design clothes, shoes and so much more.

17. E-NEWSLETTERS FOR SMALL SPECIALISED BUSINESSES

In the past newsletters were printed on paper; today PDF's are the rave! Best of all there is no capital outlay today.Most people have a computer with a basic word processing program. All you need to do is gather the specialist information including articles and pictures, and then send it all out per email. Many companies are becoming increasingly aware of the importance of networking and social media presence. Combining a clever newsletter that is sent electronically that has some 'take-home' value in it will always work.

You can offer to run the entire thing, from creation to sending out, or just to the layout and design. Couple this with photographic and computer skills and you may soon be creating a number of newsletters for various smaller specialist companies. As your reputation and the size of your newsletter subscriptions increase, companies will start offering you money to advertise in these newsletters!

18. FIVERR.COM

Are you good at designing anything? And you can do it relatively fast? Visit www.fiverr.com and see what people are doing for $5. Now add your service and make extra money on the side. You may get a few laughs when you visit the site and see what people do, but I have used many of the service providers here to design logos, do SEO reports and even set up web sites. There are people that will create portraits, caricatures and do all sorts of stuff for you. This site is become more and more popular and definitely a site where you can make money of the side if you offer the right service.

19. FUNKY INVOICES

Don't laugh at this idea! Consider for a moment a finance department in a big firm. On a daily basis they receive invoice that need to be paid. Most are standard template invoices and some have unique company logos on them, but in general they all look the same. Now imagine one of these companies had a query about a payment. When they phone the finance department, they have to quote an invoice number, and the admin clerk will then try locate said invoice.

There is no way that this admin clerk will remember this invoice, especially as they are all the same. Imagine offering a service where you created funny, funky and different invoices for clients. Invoices that have funny pictures on them, are designed completely differently to any other invoices. All still contain the basic essential information, yet the design stand out. I am part of a Master Mind Group and years ago we came up with the idea that our invoices need to be different.

My invoice is in my corporate colours, black and gold, has a picture of it of a small man pulling a large sack of money with the wording, 'Early payment appreciated'! It is not your standard white, green or pink! The picture is funny. When the finance clerk pics up the invoice, they immediately smile because of the funny cartoon picture. Guess what? When I phone and ask about my payments the clerk immediately laughs and remembers my invoice. Guess what, odds are my invoice never gets lost and I always get paid. See the psychology behind this? So how about designing your own funky invoices and selling these to companies with the premise of having their accounts settles sooner because of being different! Important! Make sure the first funky invoice you design is your own one!

20. GREETING CARDS

When last have you bought a birthday card for someone, or in fact any special occasion card? Have you noticed how expensive they have become? Office supply stores sell really good quality card that most printers can handle. Design some unique cards 9most DTP software even have built in templates) and market these to gift stores and your social circle at a lower cost than the current offerings in stores. Also, offer to customise cards and do one-off personalised prints; this will open a niche market for you. In fact you can offer a phone in service. Have the card designs displayed on your website and clients can phone in/email before 10h00 in the morning and collect the personalised card at 17h00 on the same day!

21. HUMOROUS SIGNS FOR THE HOME & WORKPLACE

I love humour and funny sayings, in fact I post these daily on my Facebook page and have been doing so for years. I started my career as a comedy entertainer, and still do live appearances. Hence this is a special subject for me. I still have an old file of photocopied jokes and cartoons that I converted to digital. Using your imagination, coupled with good DTP software, you can create great posters with funny sayings, or redraw funny pictures and cartoons and create PDF books, or one-off posters that people can buy. You can even bring out a series of these under a certain topic or company theme. Create funny bar-signs for home bars. Stickers for cars, silly sayings to hang from your car rear-view mirror. The sky is the limit!

22. ICONS & SYMBOLS

Do a search on the Internet for social media icons and symbols. You will find tons of designs. Why not create your own but also brand them for companies. Now a corporate has a familiar Facebook icon, yet it has their branding in it and is unique. People with webpages may want to imbed these symbols, but would prefer something different. There is a big market in taking standard symbols and icons and creating recognisable, yet slightly different designs. Companies and SME's will pay you good money for this.

23. ID CARDS

Where do I start? Every club, association and many companies have ID cards for members and staff members. Granted, today some have computer chips embedded in them and look like bank credit cards. However, there are still many institutions that are quite happy with a simple laminated card. Some may have barcode scanners to scan the cards, and these can easily be printed on the back of the card when you create it on your computer. It's a case of coming up with some funky designs and approaching people that may have use of this. Have basic templates where you can just drop in the club/association/company logo and all the personal details with photo.

24. LANDSCAPE DESIGNING

There is software available for this, or you can do it by hand! In fact you even have software to design and furnish rooms in houses. Many people cannot visualise or be creative enough to do this on their own. If you have an eye, plus the right software, you can create magic for them. Advertise on the Internet with examples and word of mouth will grow your business.

25. LAMINATION SERVICE

Laminating has been around for year and has somehow not become dated. Most stationary stores will sell you a laminator for well under $100. You may even have one stored in a cupboard somewhere! The laminate pockets can be bought in various sizes and come in packs of 50, 100 and more. Parents want to preserve their child's drawings, people want to laminate certificates and other important documents. How about offering an inclusive service where you scan said documents/pictures etc, laminate them and also supply the DVD with the digital files on them. A fully comprehensive service that you can charge a fair price for rendering. Most people want to sort out their documents, photos etc offer to create a DVD with everything digitally stored. You then design a template onto which you stick the photos/ documents/drawings and laminate these accordingly. The client now has all their precious documents sorted, stored and preserved. Your CD label and laminate label has a catchy design and all your contact details.

26. LOGO DESIGN

A quick search on the Internet will bring up numerous software that creates logos. In fact there are even free logo design websites you can visit and create various logos. Now combine this software with a creative imagination where you tweak and adjust the software logo, making it uniquely your own and you have a new business venture. EVERY business wants their own logo. Maybe you already have a creative imagination and a feel for logos. All you need is a basic DTP program that allows you to draw and away you go. PhotoShop is the ideal program for this. Even CoreDraw is awesome. Create some unique logos and approach various businesses in your area. Ideally start with the small one or two man businesses that can't afford professional ad agencies to create designs. Offer then a good special deal that is affordable. Once you have created logos for a few smaller companies you have earned credibility to approach bigger companies. And so you build your brand and reputation.

27. MAGNETIC VEHICLE SIGNS

Office supply stores sell adhesive magnetic sheets in various paper sizes and rolls. You can print any logo design, stick it to a magnetic sheet and you have a vehicle sign. Not good for wet weather though, so

I would recommend you design the sign and have a specialist printer do the finished waterproof magnetic sign for you. There are tons of SME's out there that cannot afford expensive advertising. If you come it at an affordable rate and offer to design flashy magnetic vehicle signs, there should be a huge demand. Just take a drive around today and see how few cars actually have such signs on their door. The market is untapped and very large. Yes, it will take active door to door marketing, but hey, start with your own magnetic signs on your own car that advertise your service. Some initial target markets would be plumbers, driving schools, electricians; carpenters, entertainers, bands etc.

28. MENUS

The scope with any DTP software is huge! Every restaurant has a menu and often these need to be replaced on a regular basis. Come up with a few clever designs, from standard prints to laminated copies. Approach restaurants in your area and offer to design and print their menus. Include add on colour-in and game pages that they can give to young children to keep them occupied while waiting for the food. Depending on the restaurant, you could even couple this with a competition and offer to manage this for them too.

29. NEWSLETTER/LEAFLET PRINTING/DISTRIBUTION SERVICE

I hate spam in my mailbox and I am not referring to email advertising, but the hundreds of leaflets that appear in my post box daily; from supermarket products, electronics to home services. If anything, I would have thought that with the advent of electronic advertising, that leaflets would have fallen in popularity. If anything, there are now more than ever before! Once again, with a simple free open source DTP program it is relatively easy to design a leaflet. A good laser printer prints many leaflets at low cost, enabling you to offer a leaflet design and print service for smaller quantities at competitive prices. If you have a brother, sister, friend that has the time, you could even quote extra and have them deliver these s required.

30. NOVELTY AD AGENCY TO PROMOTE BUSINESSES IN YOUR AREA

Print technology today makes it affordable for the majority of people today to create impressive novelty items, from printing on blank pens, matchbooks, car disk holders, key rings, rulers, calendars and so much more. Most stationary and arts & crafts stores have these items readily at hand. Come up with witty quotations, poems and drawings that highlight a product and/or its features. Personalise items around the characteristics of people within a company and package everything in a unique manner. Create general novelty items and approach novelty stores to sell them for you.

Join networking groups where various business representatives are in regular attendance. Use these events to show, talk about and promote your new ideas. Yes, you may need some start up capital, but today you can create unique one or two off items that won't cost you an arm and a leg. These are all you need to show to potential buyers. They then place orders and that's how you build the business. Once companies see that you think out of the box, they could soon approach you to take over all their marketing business. The potential is huge!

31. NOVELTY PASSPORT / ID PHOTOS

Have you checked out the prices of Passport and ID photos? The market is huge, including photos for membership cards at societies and clubs. All you need is a decent digital camera, some basic lighting and ideally a portable printer with guillotine so that you can print and cut out the photos there and then. Yes, many photographic stores offer this service in malls and high streets, but a portable service could just be a novel idea. Why not think out of the box and approach busy embassies or government departments and strike a deal which includes renting space to do this. What about a huge sports event such as a marathon where everyone needs a photo; approach the organisers and try be the official ID photographer!

32. PERSONALISED STORYBOOKS FOR CHILDREN

How the world has changed! Years ago you needed a literary agent who would approach publishers with your ideas. I believe many budding authors lost out big time! I know a number of people who have actually written a few short children's stories and always talk of publishing them 'one day'! Here is your chance. With the advent of technology you now have POD publishing; print on demand publishing. This changes everything! In fact you can visit https://kdp.amazon.com/en_US which is amazon's publishing arm. Here you can create a free account and have your own book published on amazon!

You need to download their templates and create your book in Word and convert it to a pdf. Design a cover and also convert this to pdf. Now upload it all and you have a book. Most cities have printers that do this

POD publishing. You need to supply them with the pdf inside and cover and they can print from 1 to 1000 copies. Yes, they can print even one copy only! And at a cheap price. This means you can create a children's story book and offer to have them personalised with the child's name on the cover and as the main character in the stories. If you know Word or any word processing program, it's a case of selecting, "Find and Replace' in the original text and the name is changed! Your start up costs are your time and learning to do the layout. Once you have learnt this, you market your services and away you go.

33. PHOTO BOOKS

Years ago this was unheard of, and only something the super rich could afford. Today every Mac computer has iPhoto installed which has this feature built in. You design your own photo book and order right from within the software; world-wide! In fact with the advent of POD publishing (Publishing on Demand) many printers now offer free software for you to design your own photo book and they print it within a few days at a minimal cost. Not everyone is creative in designing such a book and laying out the photos in a creative way. You could offer this service for a fee and still have a deal with the printer that he gives you a referral commission.

34. PLACEMAT SERVICE

Do you have placemats in your kitchen that you bought from a home store? Now imagine having personalised placemats – even ones that have family photos on them, or catchy quotations! I came across this idea years ago when I wanted to buy placemats for my bar counter in my home. Something came up and I ended up working with old photos when the idea struck me to create a montage of photos in PhotoShop on a A3 size page, add a nice frame and print everything. At the time I had a A3 size printer (that's double the size of a normal A4/letter page). These I then laminated, as I had an old laminating machine in a cupboard. Suddenly I had a really cool personal placemat! In fact many tourist shops sell exactly that – a large photo laminated as a placemat. Now I can change my placemats regularly.

As friends would visit, they asked who made these placemats for me. Guess what, I started offering to make the same for them, at a fee! This grew into a nice sideline business. Then as a speaker who attends many corporate functions I noticed that many where themed events and the table decorations all complimented the theme. Suddenly I had the idea to create placemats for corporate events and even included names at the tables. It's a unique concept and with the right conference and event organisers behind you, this can become a booming business.

35. POSTERS FOR DOWNLOAD

As an inspirational speaker, I share quotations with people regularly (www.wolfgangriebe.com). At one point I started creating JPEG pictures on PhotoShop and would post both the written and the pic version of this quotation on my social media sites. Why? Some people prefer the written word, but others prefer pictures. Hence the jpeg pic could be shared quickly and easily – and is visual. During a Master Mind Group brainstorm a fellow speaker suggested selling these pics in either a calendar format, or as a series of posters. This is how the idea grew into a good sideline business. You don't need to do quotations, it can be anything that appeals to people, even pictures. Create them as high quality psd's on PhotoShop and now offer them as downloads on you e-commerce site. You can sell them individually or as groups of pics. Once you have designed the pic and uploaded it onto the site; the rest becomes automated.

36. PUBLISHING

If you visit www.mindpowerpublications.com you will see that this is my own publishing company. I have done exactly what I am describing to you here. Firstly, I researched how the publishing industry works in terms of book creation, layout and design. I found out about self publishing on www.amazon.com and www.lulu.com, plus read as many articles as I could on the net. I also attended a lecture one evening that was advertised in the local newspaper on publishing. Then I started creating my own books. Soon I noticed that speakers in my industry didn't have the time nor drive to do what I did. Furthermore, journalists don't really like reviewing 'self published' books.

Hence I took a problem and created an opportunity. I searched for a nice available domain name and print all my and other books under this title. Now it looks like a big publishing house is the publisher. It's still only me! As I learnt how to do a layout and where to market the books, I offered this service to other speakers at a fair price and gave them a chance to have a publisher print their books. In this way we helped each other and I started building a nice sideline business.

So what stops you from approaching colleagues, specialists in a field and beginning the same concept? You charge a fee for the layout and design and leave the original author with the full rights of the book. But in turn request that you can sell the electronic format on your own website; this then creates a nice additional income. SEO your site correctly and build your customer base from there.

37. RELIGIOUS PARAPHERNALIA

Regardless of you religion, this can be a huge business. Whether it's booklets with bible verses, bookmarks, puzzles or posters with religious quotations, this market is massive. Just take Christianity and Muslims alone; you are talking about more than a billion people! So what's stopping you designing something for the religious market?

38. SCREEN PRINTING

This has been around for years, and odds are it will be around for many more. Screen printing is relatively easy to do and cheap to set up. However you can print on all sorts of surfaces and for anyone that is creative, this is almost like a photographer who still develops his own film in a dark room – you have artistic license and its hands on. One idea is to come up with creative designs and print them on material using screen printing, now you can sell this designer material or even make your own style of clothes with it. A designer range of T-Shirts with your own sayings on it is also an idea. In fact many art stores sell start up screen printing kits and these give you a great idea of the possibilities available.

39. SERVICE PRINTERS

Companies are launching new printers and new versions of printers daily. Even though they may look more modern, the basics inside remains fairly constant. Many people throw printers away because they don't realise that all they need is a good clean of the wheels and cogs inside. Often ink gets caught up on the inside and this affects print quality. Once you understand how most printers work, a service could take as short as ten minutes and the client has a new printer again. Alternatively go on a course offered by one of the manufacturers on servicing their printers – it is really worth the knowledge you gain!

40. SIGNAGE

Signs are everywhere! And yes they all look the same. Use your Photoshop skills and create funky, different designs for standard signage such as warning signs, information signs and even 'ladies ' & 'gents' signs. Offer these to restaurants and business in your area. A new commercial property or even shop may be being built right now in your suburb. Who is it? Find out and offer to do their signage at a special price. Every building has signs, from warning to information signs and these cost a lot of money. Do your research and find the right card/ plastic to make these signs. By adding the 'different' creative touch, you can get ahead of the competition. What about custom signage? All signs look the same, but if you offer to have the company logo or name on each sign, it now personalises everything for that company. I would much rather have a personalised sign in my offices than a standard off-the-shelf sign.

41. SHEET MUSIC

Sheet music has always been very expensive. Today there is software that writes music for you. Consider putting together music books using a spiral binder. A spiral binder opens up nicely on the music stand and is actually ideal for music sheets. Compile themed music books, individual songs and even teaching books. Approach music schools and people in the industry. I have a daughter that plays piano and see the prices the music stores charge. If you can approach music schools/ teachers and put together a personalised music book for them that they sell to students, you could be onto something good here!

42. SPECIAL OCCASION PRINTING

The list is endless, but here are some special occasions where someone may need some creative help and you can design that special memory of print that will make the occasion unforgettable. Marriage proposals, engagement, promotions, anniversary, special announcement, etc! For example, a young man may be looking for a unique way to ask his girlfriend to become engaged. You may have printed a special photo book for a couple where the last page has a marriage proposal printed in it. You could use a similar idea for this man. This is a specialist job and the more creative you can be with your print ideas, the better. Just remember that most people get engaged/ married/promoted etc. With the right branding and reputation this can become a booming business.

43. STENCILS/PICS FOR CHILDREN'S ROOMS

When my daughters where small I painted their rooms with fairy-tale figures. Many people are not artistic and cannot recreate a cartoon drawing. Years ago an overhead projector worked well. Today one can project a picture onto the wall with a digital data projector and draw over the outline in order to get the picture right. All these methods are complicated. So why not design stick on basic pictures that parents can use, or even better, create a template of   well-known cartoon characters that can just be traced. Children are born everyday, this is a market that will never become dated!

44. STICKERS

A question; have you seen the stick figure families that many cars have stuck of their rear windows. Someone came up with the idea and now they are world-wide. What is stopping you from coming up with a clever sticker design that could be the next global craze. Adhesive paper is cheap to buy and odds are you already own a printer. Let your creative juices flow and come up with a number of novel designs for stickers. Show them to your family and social circle and get feedback. They could be a figment of your imagination or even related to some local, international or political event. Start with a sticker on your car and see how many people request one as well. Alternatively market them in stationary and gift shop stores and on the Internet.

45. T-SHIRTS

Clever sayings, play on words and funny lines are huge on T-shirts. If you can design your own funky brand, i.e. a special frame on the front with your website printed in the frame, and then add a clever picture of saying in the frame, you suddenly have your own brand of T-Shirts. Just when I think I have seen it all, someone else comes up with a clever design. One can tailor make T-Shirts for corporate events. The market is huge. If you have your own unique idea, it's not going to cost that much to print a started range and have friends wear them and spread the brand. Just be careful not to infringe on any brand names or copyrights.

46. TEMPLATES

Look at your DTP software. The most popular is Microsoft office at the moment. Open a new Word document and you have the option of selecting a document from a number of available templates. This saves you time and makes your life easier. So how about designing your own templates and offering these for sale on the internet. I know one company that designs 'transition' templates for video editors on Motion and After Effects. Every month he designs new templates and regularly offers specials. These are made available on an e-commerce website. He is doing very well. You may have a knack at designing PowerPoint slides, or Newsletter designs. Build a free e-commerce website using Prestashop (installed on most web servers) and offer your templates at fair prices to a world market. It's all about being creative and different! Do a search on popular software and see what's available already. Find one where there is a need for more templates and build on this.

47. TRAINING & OTHER MANUALS

Many companies do not have the time or motivation to create and update their training manuals, standard operating procedures and other important manuals. Become creative, and design some easy to read templates. Then simply insert their information into your ready-made templates. You can then add a follow-up service to keep these updated as well. Charge extra if they want you to sift through the material and compile everything for them. Companies usually supply you with everything, and you merely make it all look nice! In terms of updating certain manuals, they need to give you the relevant websites where updates are posted. These you monitor and then apply the updates when and how they occur – and charge accordingly.

48. WEBPAGES DESIGN

Recently I updated a website of mine and was searching through the templates at WordPress - there are hundreds! Yet I couldn't find a free one that I liked. Then I ended up on a site that sells templates, and suddenly I found what I liked. If you understand websites and are clued up on Wordpress, Joomla, PrestaShop etc create your own templates and sell them online.

49. WEDDING STATIONERY

Technology has made the wedding stationary business more accessible than ever before. Even though Publishing on Demand has become extremely popular (Small quantity printing), the average person can create beautiful stationary on a basic home computer and printer. Laser printers have become so much cheaper over the last few years and a variety of grained paper is available on which to print. All you need is a basic desk top publishing set up with the right software (there is even a large selection of 'open source' [free] software available on the Internet). Come up with some creative designs, and share these with all your friends who intend getting married. You can advertise at specialist wedding stores and focus on 'smaller' weddings offering an exclusive service. Check out current pricing so that you remain competitive. The wedding market is huge and many people make lots of money in the wedding business. Therefore if you have a good value for money product; this can grow into a big business very quickly.

50. WINE LABELS

Imagine receiving a gift bottle of wine with your own unique label on it. A few years back this was a sideline home business that could be done using a home printer. However, both inkjet and laser printing are not ideal, as the paper stock you print on is limited, and the ink may run if wet. Today with POD publishing companies springing up everywhere, you can easily have a professional label or 2 printed for cheap.

You need to be good at designing in order to create a clever label. Then you can either take photos of the person concerned, or have spouses/ family members send you the photos they want on the label. Never forget that a simple idea like this can make lots of money!

> *Never apologise for having high standards. People who really want to be in your life will rise up to meet them.*

YOUR OWN DESIGN & PRINT HOME BUSINESS IDEAS

HANDYMAN SUPPLY & FIT

50 Home Business Ideas you can do with as a DIY handyman. There are a number of bigger jobs that require no capital upfront if you get the customer to give you a 50% deposit before starting the job. You use the money to purchase everything you need and the rest is then pure profit. This is typically your 'Supply & Fit' type of work. Many men already have most of the tools in their garages if they are keen handymen, so here is a great opportunity to really offer specialised services that can bring in excellent incomes on the side and easily become full time jobs.

1. APPLIANCE REPAIR SERVICE

Like most men, I can take the cover off an electrical item and look if there is a loose wire. Besides that I am no good with electronic items. However, there are many people who have a keen interest and are quite clued up on the workings of a washing machine, microwave, stove, vacuum cleaner and toaster.

Often when one of these breaks, it requires a quick fix and everything is in order again. If you call the company that made the product, their representative has a steep call out fee, and if they do repair the product, the total costs are usually not much less that if you buy a new item – hence many people tend to throw out appliances that break. Here's where you come in – start in your neighbourhood so that you don't have to charge crazy call out fees! Start with basic repairs. As you become proficient and see what items break the most, build up your supplier contacts. Build up your customer base on recommendations and work well done.

2. BOAT CLEANING SERVICE

So, you always wanted to live by a lake, ideally in a holiday resort, yet there are very few jobs available to keep the money coming in, and it is seasonal. Here's an idea that can keep you busy all year round! If you are at the coast, even better, as the salt in the sea air will require more regular boat cleaning. If you have, or ever have had a boat, the worst part of owning one is cleaning it after use. Also, you need to look at the hull and maintain it regularly. Many resorts have 'boat parking garages' where the boats are stored out of season. Wow – an ideal place to start offering a cleaning service.

Regardless of where it is, boat owners all need to maintain their boats. What better time to do it than out of season. Maybe you own a guest house or even a restaurant in a resort, and out of season you pull your hair out to cover costs. Here's your answer! Once people know that you offer a reliable and efficient cleaning service you will have a regular stream of customers. Plus the bonus is that they have to maintain these boats on a regular basis, which means that once you have a customer, odds are they remain a customer for as long as they own that boat!

3. CAR ALARMS AND CAR RADIO CD/DVD PLAYERS

Do you have a good knowledge of electronics, especially car electronics? Then this could be a good possibility. Make sure you find a reputable supplier of quality products and start out by doing the installations at people's homes. As the business builds up you could always move into a premises. Ideally though, it could be a niche market if you operate the business as a mobile one. Start by advertising what you do to your social circle and in your neighbourhood and build it up from there.

4. CARPENTRY

Are you a skilled carpenter? No you don't need a full-time job on a building site. There are may opportunities all around you. People need doors aligned or planed shorter due to swelling. Kitchen cupboard doors are out of alignment. Drawers don't work properly anymore. You can go to 99% of homes and find these problems. Offer to fix these at reasonable rates. Some people may require something build from wood, wether it is a children's jungle jim, a book shelf, a wall unit, bar or even a trap door in the ceiling. These are all skills most carpenters should have. If you are not a carpenter, these are skills you can learn pretty quickly by attending various short course. From making pet travel boxes, to children's toys and dollhouses – the scope is endless if you have carpentry skills.

5. CARPETS: SUPPLY & CLEAN

If you are a practical person and the do-it-yourself type, then you can basically tackle anything. Although carpet laying is something you need to learn, it's really not that difficult to do. Initially you could find a reputable company and simply add a commission on top of their price. Be at the job when they fit the carpet and watch and learn until you can eventually do it all yourself. The goal would be to eventually have your own van as carpets to need to collected.

What about cleaning carpets? The machines can be hired and one can easily do an average house in a morning. Most people don't have the time and if your fees are reasonable, then carpet cleaning can become a good extra income.

6. CHILDREN'S JUNGLE GYMS

These are timber frames, usually made from timber poles, in various designs where children can play on. Some have a section with swings attached. Others may have a small roof over one section and even a slide on another section. The size and features can all depend on the budget the client has available. We had one built in our garden when my daughters where 4 and they played on it until about age 12. Once you have made a few template designs it easy to buy the timber from a supplier and you can literally put it up within a morning. I had a friend who started this and within a year he was exporting his jungle gyms overseas!

7. COFFEE TABLES

Do yourself a favour and price coffee/living room tables at a furniture store. I couldn't believe the cost. If you are handy with wood work, or metal work, here is a really novel idea. The basics of these coffee tables is that the glass top has items underneath it. In essence you are construct a tray/drawer with 4 legs and a piece of glass on top. Basically it's like a picture frame/display case on legs! So instead of a normal wooden or tiles table top, they look into the table top and see various items below. The depth of the table top depends on what you put in it. I have seen tables with a collection of shells that looked stunning. In fact you could even use a painting. Do you want to know what to do with your old vinyl records – create a table top with them and cover it with glass. You are limited to your imagination. A friend of mine made a table with all the old nuts and bolts in his garage – it looked stunning!

8. CONVERT JUNK INTO ART AND FURNITURE

In my profession as a trainer and speaker, I get to appear at a variety of resorts and venues where people can listen to what I have to say. This gives me huge exposure to venues throughout the world. Since about 2010 I have noticed many wine estates converting old barns to restaurants and conference venues. Recently I was at a place where they had hung an old upright piano from the ceiling (obviously removed the insides). Half way up the wall they had fastened an old wooden music centre cabinet. Everywhere I looked there was an old 50's'60's'70' piece of furniture that they had repainted, hung, fastened somewhere in this barn. It almost looked like an artists warehouse! It worked! It looked brilliant! All the items were furniture that was broken, old and not being used.

These were things people dump on their pavement for the council to collect, or at junkyards. By using your imagination you could take these old items and paint them in bright colour, cut two in half and stick mismatching pairs together, frame and old plate... the sky is the limit.

Offer this as 'alternative' decorations. By the trend I have seen around the world – this could be a very profitable business.

9. CORNICES, MOULDINGS AND SKIRTING BOARDS

Today, this has become so easy to do. Years ago putting up cornices was a huge mess as the CreteStone used as the adhesive is incredibly messy. The preparation took time. Today with pre-moulded polystyrene and a flexible acrylic adhesive it takes literally 3 minutes to put up a 2 meter length. The only skill is to learn how to cut the angles for the corners... which is actually easy to do with the right tools. Skirting boards are mostly wood, but easy to work with as it's floor level. This job takes hardly any investment, and can be started up overnight. Changing plain cornices into lavish moulded cornices is simply a case of sticking the new ones over the old ones and it makes a huge difference to a room. You would basically be charging a labour rate only, as the material is fairly cheap, which also means that it is affordable to many more people. This means you can easily find jobs as well.

10. CRIME SCENE CLEAN UP SERVICE

I never even knew such a job existed! A friend of mine told me she had done this part time a few years ago and that it was an extremely lucrative job that very few people wanted to do. After doing some research on the subject I can confirm that this is indeed a specialist job with huge growth potential.   Crime is on the increase world-wide, murders suicides, accidents and many other incidents that result in human blood and other fluids remaining at the scene, need to be cleaned up. Besides the emotional trauma, there is a danger from exposure to blood borne pathogens that can be infectious. Think about it, once the police and all relevant authorities have left the scene – someone has to clean it up!

This can usually only be done manually. In other words, people physically have to go in and clean up and disinfect the area. Approach your local police stations and find out what training is required. Do an apprenticeship with a company already doing this. You wear hazard suits so no bodily fluids come near you. It is highly controlled and you can charge for ever cloth and bit of clean up material you use. You will need training and of course safe ways of disposing of the waste material. The majority of people find blood and body parts disturbing. Some people are quite comfortable with this. If you are one of them, and don't mind being called out at any hour of the day – this is an extremely lucrative job!

11. DOORS

To hang a door is a learnt skill. Find a carpenter that can do this and learn from them. A background in woodwork will help as well. Many people struggle to fit their own doors and never get it right. Whether it's hanging a door, replacing one or trimming a door down, the opportunities are out there. Once you know how to do it and have the right tools, it is an easy in and out job. However, be careful of steel door frames where the hinges have rusted off – that becomes a problem and you may have to weld, or rivet new hinges onto the frame. Always check first before quoting, as this takes more time.

12. ELECTRIC SHOWERS

Hot water cylinders cost money and electricity has become expensive world-wide. Many people are searching for alternatives in order to save on electricity costs. An electric shower is one of those alternatives. If you are experiences as an electrician and have some plumbing skills, this is a relatively easy and quick installation compared to plumbing a whole bathroom. Find a good supplier and market your services in your neighbourhood first.

13. ELECTRICAL LEADS

Find a supplier or manufacturer who can supply you in bulk at discounted prices. Put together sets of extension leads in various sizes and number of sockets. e.g. long leads with one socket for gardeners and do-it-yourselfers, 2-way and 4-way sockets for indoor electrical appliances etc. If you're a whiz at soldering, you might also consider producing a variety of audio and video leads. Package your products in cellophane bags with a stapled header card advertising your product and business name. Sell through hardware stores or market stall.

14. ELECTRICAL REPAIRS AND INSTALLATIONS INCLUDING LIGHTS

As electricity costs soar, some people want to replace their current light bulbs with energy saving bulbs or LED lights. Bigger houses means that this is a timeous exercise. Find a good supplier and offer the lights at a premium rate, with your profit included and then work out a cost per bulb. Believe me, most husbands put this job off as long as they can. Include a basic electrical repair and check service in this. In other words you will repair faulty plugs and switches as well. These are the jobs most people find time wasters and don't take priority in many homes. If you have a good package deal for the average home, this can be a huge money spinner.

15. FENCE REPAIR

Most properties, residential and commercial, have fences or some form of security fence around them. From wood to steel, these all need to be installed and then maintained. Wooden fences need regular varnishes or painting. Steel fences need occasional repair and parts replaced. Today with security become an increasing concern, particularly for commercial property, they also need maintenance! You could even offer to install fencing and couple with with a 5 year maintenance contract! Do yourself a favour and take a drive through any suburb and through any commercial and industrial area. Who is maintaining all those fences? Unless you are installing them, the mere maintenance of fencing does not require much start-up capital. Recommendations and service well done can build your name very quickly.

16. FIBRE GLASS MODELS FOR COMMERCIAL USE

Working with fibre-glass can be extremely creative and you are only limited to your imagination in terms of creating shapes. From large hamburgers to small models of cars, anything can be made with fibre-glass and used as a promotional gimmick outside a shop of factory. You will need an empty garage space at least, and one that's well ventilated to start your business. Market your services in commercial and industrial areas to get the business off the ground.

17. FIT GAS FIRES AND DECORATIVE FIRE PLACES

As climate change increases, winters are getting colder. Electric and coal fires are becoming expensive to run, hence gas is a good alternative. If this interests you and you have no experience, find part time work with someone that does this kind of work. The bigger profits come from those people that simply want a decorative fire place for show.

18. FIT CUSTOM CAR PRODUCTS

The sky is really the limit here... from fitting alloy wheels, special graphics and lettering, hard-drive & LCD screens to special body kits. I would suggest keeping to 'clean' items that don't involve grease and oil, in other words, stay aways from the mechanical. You want to supply and fit items that can go quick and easy with a fast turn around, thus increasing your profits. Again, a simple course or a keen interest in the above will enable you to do this pretty quickly.

19. GRAFFITI REMOVAL

Sadly, this is a growing problem in cities and filtering down into smaller towns. Most councils cannot cope with the problem, plus property owners in industrial and residential areas are increasingly being targeted as well. Many private home owners find it extremely difficult to remove graffiti, whether it be from cement, wood or steel. As a handyman, what you cannot clean, you can replace! Hence you are in the pound seats. Find out what cleaning materials are available and do your research. Simply approaching private people whose properties have been vandalised is going to keep you busy on its own.

Add the local council and you could build up a big business. If there are areas that are regularly vandalised with graffiti, offer a bi-monthly clean-up fee. To build up a base of clients where you have regular monthly cleaning is a realistic possibility. They no longer have to worry about the graffiti and you have a regular job. This you can build into a fairly big business with a team of cleaners working for you. Be aware that you will need some serious industrial cleaning materials – so make sure that you and your staff don't breath in damaging fumes. Be aware of safety at all times.

20. HEADBOARDS FOR BEDS IN TRADITIONAL AND CLASSIC DESIGNS

Here is something many people never think of – making money from headboards. Do yourself a favour and look around the homes of people you know – not many have headboards. Maybe the master suite, but most of the single beds don't. You can start with wooden headboards and as you become experienced, make padded ones. Later on you can even offer to make the whole bed with headboard and market your own unique designs.

21. HUSBAND FOR HIRE

This is, in my opinion, one of the best ideas in this book for a male. In fact, if you are a Do It Yourself female, this could really be novel too as a 'Wife with Skills for Hire.' This is all above board! Consider how many wives constantly nag their husbands to do a simple odd job. Think of the simple jobs that require only basic skills and knowledge, that most people do not have. Furniture repairing, simple plumbing, washing cars, sharpening lawnmower blades, fixing simple electrical appliances such as kettles and toasters, fitting cupboards and shelves, etc. Any library will have self study books and if you are practically minded, advertise yourself as a handyman, or woman, and you could be kept very busy. One man I knew advertised himself in the local classifieds as "Husband for Hire". Very novel and today he has a few guys working for him as they cannot keep up with demand.

22. INTERNET

Many people do not know how to set up the Internet in their homes, never mind WiFi. You may already have the knowledge, or you can attend a really short basic course to learn how to do this. You will be surprised at how many people cannot do this. Advertise your services in your area and at old age homes. Many elderly want to stay in touch with their children. Learn how to do it on both Windows and Macintosh and have a fair priced basic call-out fee. Don't limit yourself to desktop computers, but include tablets and mobile phones as well. It shouldn't take you more than 30 – 45 minutes to do a connection. Once you build up a name you can offer various other IT related services from installing software to setting up emails and even web pages. The sky is the limit!

23. INTERIOR DECORATOR

Some may argue that this doesn't fall under the handyman service – I beg to differ. You may be a practical person that is extremely good at DIY projects, plus have a great eye for novel and unique designs. You may be one of those people that can take a piece of junk and make something awesome out of it and sell it for ten times it's worth. Have you walked into someone's home and thought to yourself, "Man I could do so much more with this room?" Couple this with carpentry, metal and artistic skills and you could be embarking on an amazingly creative and lucrative idea. Couple this with a knowledge of where to buy all the interesting items with which to do up a room or home, and you are ready to embark on a new career!

24. LOFT INSULATION SERVICE

People need to try everything to save on electrical and heating costs. Most heat escapes through the roof, hence the need to insulate a loft. Realistically, the loft is dusty, full of creepy crawly insects such as spiders, and not an area of the house that most people frequent. If you don't mind cramped spaces with some insects; there is a big market to do these installations.

25. MOBILE CAR/BIKE SERVICE

Here's my gripe with taking my car in for a service... that's the gripe – I have to take it in. Even if the dealer gives me a courtesy car; it's still takes time out of my daily schedule. Granted, the majority of new vehicles come with services plans and need an IT specialist, rather than a mechanic to service them. It appears as if you just plug in a laptop and it's all done via computer! Seriously though, many people still have older vehicles that need to be serviced the traditional way, i.e. change the oil, plugs etc.

If you specialise in some of the popular older brands and offer to do this after hours and over weekends at the person's home – or even during office hours at the company parking lot (this will bring in lots of extra work from surrounding companies) you have a niche market. Create a clever portable kit for yourself with enough stock of oil, plus & tools and target people with older cars. This could realistically expand very fast with you employing other mechanics and maybe even starting a franchise!

26. MOBILE EXHAUST SERVICE

Time is money and unless someone has an exhaust fitting dealership near their place of work, it's always a mission to take the car in and have this done. If you are an experienced mechanic, how about offering to do this at the client's home or office? Offer a mobile exhaust fitting service. When they phone you get the make and model of the car and simply fetch everything from the supplier as you make your way to the client. In this way you don't carry stock and offer a specialised service where your profits come from your labour costs.

27. MOBILE WELDING SERVICE

If you have any experience using industrial welding equipment, particularly where motorists are concerned, this should be easy. There are always a fair number of people who need welding repairs carried out on their car or van. How many simple household items break that require 5 minutes of welding? The market is huge. With suitable portable equipment and a large enough van to contain it, this is a business which has no shortage of customers for those with the necessary skills. Make sure your welding machine is portable and always protect your surroundings from sparks when working indoors.

28. NEW KITCHEN IN A DAY

Let's be realistic, most people would love a new kitchen, but the costs are just too high. Besides, it takes time and is really messy. Imagine you could offer a 'new kitchen in a day' service that involved minimal mess? This is nothing new, but so few people do it, simply replace all the cupboard doors! Ask yourself this question, what takes the most time when building a new kitchen? It's the cupboards. Granted, many cupboard may be old inside, but a good clean with proper cleaning materials can do wonders. Cover the current shelf with a washable adhesive paper and you pretty much have a refurbished cupboard. All you need to do now is add new doors and the kitchen looks great.

Decide on the finishes at your first visit and take all the measurements. Have everything cut to size and come in for a day and replace the doors – a new kitchen in a day! There are a number of firms who can supply these doors at trade prices, allowing you to charge for your fitting service on top of the price of the doors you supply at retail cost. Of course you can change tops, add tiles and do paintwork too. With the right team this too can be accomplished within a day. Offer to fit new stoves and fridges for a small extra fee and you have an all inclusive kitchen business! Make a point of taking before and after pictures and keep a folder on you at all times. Every house owner will call their neighbours over to have a look at the kitchen. There is no better timing to take out your folder of photos and sign up the next client!

29. OUTDOOR GARDEN FEATURES AND LIGHTING SYSTEMS

This includes pool pumps, water features using pumps, irrigation systems and garden lighting. Most people are afraid to tackle out door electrical work. If you are qualified and have the skills you will be surprised at how many people would actually utilise your services. People are forever upgrading their homes and hence a really good business to be in.

30. PATIOS AND GARDEN LAYOUTS

You don't need electrical and plumbing skills to be handyman! Basic woodwork knowledge is all you need to build wooden patios and railings. You need an artistic flair to design interesting gardens, create garden paths and come up with unique garden layouts. Once you have done your first garden, word of mouth will get your name out there.

31. PETS: WOOD DOG KENNELS AND SCRATCH POSTS FOR CATS

Have you seen the pet fashions and jewellery available for pets around the world? There is a huge market for pet products. Designing, making and supplying pet accessories, from clothes that looks funky to practical pet jerseys to keep them warm. I have even seen pet wigs! You have no idea how some people dress up their pets! That's great with me – as long as they buy everything from my shop! Just have a look at what crazy stores are available in Los Angeles! That will give you an idea as to the scope and market out there. If you want to be less outrageous, you can even design funky pet collars and dog/cat tags.

32. REFURBISH OLD DESKS

When it comes to 2nd hand desks, these can be found everywhere, from 2nd hand dealers, to pavements in cities. Many old government and corporate buildings still have stocks of desks. Many companies replace furniture every few years. To find stock is easy! How do you get rid of it again and make a good profit? Even easier! Advertising a desk as a desk isn't going to do much, but advertising an old desk that has been slightly altered and refurbished as a computer desk; now that will move. In the days of CD's and DVD's, you could just add a CD holder. When computers where still boxes, one could cut a hole in the desk and mount the computer monitor inside the desk at an angle. All these alterations cost little, but changed an old desk into a new one. What is technology doing today? How can you alter and adapt an old desk to be 'in' now? Add some clever paint or varnish techniques and you can completely change the look of an old desk.

33. ROCK POOLS & FISH PONDS

Have you ever had someone quote you to build a rock pool or pond? The prices are very high! The Internet has changed our lives and you can view many courses on YouTube on how to build a pool/pond and how to create a rock finish. When my daughters were small I didn't want to have a huge pool installed, so I asked for quotations on a smaller rock pool. I was shocked at the price. By watching various videos on the Internet I began building my own rock pool. The rock finish I managed to create by taking 4 medium pesticide containers and filling them with a 4 to 1 mix of water based paint. By pumping up the containers with the handle, I managed to create a spray effect and mixed 4 colours, (red, brown, yellow and black) onto the not-quite dry cement and create an amazing rock finish. In the end the whole pool cost me a 5th of the lowest quote I had received. Learn the skill while improving your own garden, and then show your surrounding neighbours your skills. Couple this with a 'fair' price and you could soon have a booming business!

34. ROOF REPAIR SERVICE

For most homeowners, roof repairs are inevitable when strong winds and rains occur. It can be a variety of repairs, from a loose or broken tile, rotten wood beams, loose cement or a leaking flat roof that needs new water-proofing. Flat roofs always give problems and if you can specialise in these types of roofs, there's also a huge market. For someone in the roofing business, there's always another job just around the corner. If you don't mind heights and climbing ladders and balancing on sloping roofs, the opportunity is rife.

35. SECURITY LIGHTS & LIGHTS IN GENERAL

Of all the government policies and laws 'out there', why can't they make one that stipulates one standard ceiling fitting onto which any light can connect? Have you ever bought a light and thought to yourself, "This should take 10 minutes." Only to find that you have to re-drill the connector holes in the new light fitting as it doesn't line up with the old one in your ceiling? If anything, my pet hate is connecting lights. If someone offers to do this for me a a reasonable price, I won't hesitate to give them the work. With the advent of LED lights, many people are changing their light fittings and need someone to do these installations. Of course a qualified electrician would be suitable for this, but as you are not really getting involved in the electrical side as such, it is something most practical handymen can offer as a service.

36. SECURITY LOCKS ON DOORS AND WINDOWS

No matter in which country you live, security is become a world-wide issue and a huge market. Whether you install burglar alarms, security cameras, complex computer security systems, or burglar bars on windows and doors; the market is huge. Initially you target high crime areas for obvious reasons.

37. SMOKE DETECTORS

Initially I would visit the local fire department and get statistics on fires in the area. Most residential houses don't have a fire alarm. Will you wake up in time during the night if there is a fire in your home? Will you be able to get to the kid's room and save them in time? You have basic psychological and emotional scare tactics that make it easy to sell the detectors. So customers shouldn't be hard to find. What about guest houses, hotels and companies – do they all have a fire action plan? Find a reliable wholesaler and you are in business.

38. SPAS, HOT TUBS, SHOWERS

Obviously this is something suited to an experienced plumber. If you can do brickwork, then you can even fully install hot tubs and spa's, or else just sub-contract this. This is more of a luxury market, although many middle class homes are looking into hot tubs today too. By doing the service yourself you can come in at a cheaper rate than the established companies and this alone will open the middle income market for you.

39. STONE SLABS AND WALL BRICKS FOR GARDENS

Do you have some space in your garden, or an extra garage where you can afford to make a bit of a mess? How about buying a few basic moulds and casting your own pavers and bricks. You can add oxide/pigment to color the cement and come up with your own unique range. It's hard work but once people get to know your range of slabs/pavers and bricks, you could very soon be moving into bigger premises and have a booming business.

40. TELEPHONE EXTENSION LEADS AND SOCKETS

Have you ever wanted to move your land line phone into another room? It's always a mission to extend the phone plug. Even though wireless and mobile phones are taking over, there are many people that would love to move their phones to another room, or simply a more convenient location in their home or office. Offer a line extension service as well as phones. Some people may even have the budget of a wireless phone so that you simply install a base unit at the existing point and they can then carry the phone anywhere in the house. This business idea may sound simple, but you will be surprised at the amount of people that require this service. Think about it... the telephone company always keeps you waiting, so why not offer a quick and efficient service like this?

41. TILING SERVICE

Today's DIY shops have all the tools you need to lay tiles. In fact all you need is a tile cutter, a rubber mallet, and a trowel to spread the tile cement. Yes, there is a knack to cutting tiles on a tile cutter. Test and try it out on old tiles first. After you have cut and messed up a dozen, or so, you should start getting the basic knack. Remember to keep the spread of the tile cement even and use tile spacers. There is a huge demand for good tilers. It is hard work, but if you can learn to work clean and efficiently, and at a good price, this can become a big business very quickly. If you can specialise in certain designs or even make up special designs on the side to sell as added extras – this can become a business on its own.

42. SMALL TIMBER CONSTRUCTIONS

There are a number of bigger companies that offer to install Wendy houses, garden sheds, etc. Why not approach one of them and offer to become an agent and take their approved installer course. Now you build up your own team and offer to install a range of timber constructions that can even include saunas and small chalets. Focus initially on the smaller items that don't cost much to build and can be constructed quickly. Focus on service delivery and quality in order to build up a good reputation.

43. SOLAR ENERGY INSTALLATION SERVICE

Energy has become a global problem and solar energy is the future. More and more spam is arriving in my inbox from people trying to sell me solar panel heating systems. I have noticed that many hardware stores now offer DIY kits at very reasonable prices. Again, you may or may not have knowledge of how solar systems work. If not, join a company as an apprentice and learn! Don't limit yourself to heating systems! What about cheaper lighting systems that can be easily installed. Once you completely understand the technology behind solar energy you could begin supplying everyone in your neighbourhood. Start with your own home and brag to your friends how you did it on your own. Word of mouth will do the rest.

44. SPIRAL STAIRCASES

There is always something fascinating about a spiral staircase in a home, whether it leads to a loft room or a cosy bar on another level in the home. Spiral staircases can be bought, ready made from certain steel manufacturers. Negotiate a wholesale deal and offer to install these for people in need of a staircase up into the loft, or even wealthier people looking to add a unique feature in their home. If you a qualified and can weld, why not construct the entire thing yourself.

45. TV AERIALS AND SATELLITE DISHES

This is relatively easy to do. You would need to be able to use a drill and be able to fix brackets to walls, chimneys, etc. You also need to know in which direction to aim the aerial for best reception. All components can usually be bought from DIY stores as well as wholesalers in larger quantities. This is usually a quick in and out job and includes laying the coaxial cable to a TV aerial socket.

46. UPHOLSTERY REPAIR

A nifty handyman can repair many items of furniture when it comes to the wood or the steel elements that are broken, but what about the upholstery? The Internet is full of videos that teach you how to do this. Furniture costs have soared in the last few years. 20 years ago a friend of mine in the UK offered simple covers that merely covered old chairs; he was already making a good living from this. Find an old chair somewhere and take it apart; ook how they have done it. I have found that the padding on kitchen and dining-room chairs is the first to look shabby. A staple gun, some sponge and some upholstery material is all you need and these repairs can be done fairly quickly. Just look around the houses of your social circle and you will be amazed at how many people need this service. It's not difficult to learn and the start up costs are really small.

47. WELDING SERVICE

Luckily I have a welding machine and taught myself to weld. Why do I say, "Luckily"? The amount of metal items, from balustrades, to car exhausts to gutters, it's weird how much metal there is in a home. Finding a qualified welder and having them come out to do a repair that takes 5 minutes is very costly. Most people hold off repairing steel items as they believe it is going to be messy and overly expensive. Hence, if you can get yourself a nice portable welding kit and have the right covering materials so that weld splatter doesn't burn carpets and surrounding items in the home, you can start a pretty good business fairly quickly.

Set up costs is a welder and some rods. With the right marketing in your area you will be amazed out how many people have a loose panel on a car, a rusty balustrade bar that needs replacing, a gutter bracket that is loose, etc. Yes, there are many people that weld a variety of items from home, such as chairs, tables and sculptures and yes there is a market for this too. However, someone that just focuses on metal repairs with a portable welding service – that's novel and new!

48. WOOD DOG KENNELS AND SCRATCH POSTS FOR CATS

This is a HUGE market! Did I mention that this is a huge market? All dog owners need a dog kennel. Every cat owner likes to keep their lounge suite in good condition and hence by a scratch post for their cats. Have a look what is on offer at vets and in pet shops. Now go out and improve on what there is, as a more reasonable price. Work on a few templates so that it goes quick to build the range of products you offer and just let everyone in your neighbourhood know to start with. Believe me when I say this can become a booming business. Get in with vets and pet shops and start supplying them too. You can even add rabbit hutches and bird cages. Don't forget to advertise in pet magazines and sites on the Internet.

49. WOODEN GATES IN VARIOUS SIZES

Most buildings, from commercial to residential all have a gate somewhere! Here you don't have to be a carpenter, as you can by ready-made gates from most DIY stores. Simply open a dealer account and off-you-go. Many people want to close off a garden section as they have small children that mustn't go out onto the street, and others have pets they want to keep inside. Canvass a residential area with some clever marketing and away you go!

50. WROUGHT IRON GATES & BALUSTRADES

Can you weld? It's really not that difficult and courses are readily available and inexpensive to do. Or find an engineering firm that will make up the products for you. If you have an extra garage, or space in the yard and a van to transport the materials, this can become a very lucrative business. However, this is something you would start small, and from home and eventually you would need to move into your own industrial premises. Again, I know to friends that started this and within 6 months had their premises and where doing extremely well. Steel work also allows for a lot of creativity and you could easily design your own range of products.

Take small steps every day...
and you'll get there one day.

The acquisition of knowledge doesn't mean
you're growing. Growing happens when what
you know changes how you live.

Plan your work... and work your plan!

YOUR OWN HANDYMAN HOME BUSINESS IDEAS

SERVICES OUTSIDE THE HOME

Here you will find a list of home business opportunities that you can prepare, develop, store and run from home, but which require you to deliver the final product or service at the client. Many of the ideas require skills that most people already have, or have learnt as a hobby or in a DIY capacity. Others require you to attend an inexpensive course or two to get the required skills. While a handful require an initial investment to get the business' up and running.

1. ADVENTURE OUTINGS

Offer half and full day adventure trips in and around your city. These can include 4x4 off road adventures, abseiling, advanced driving courses at a race track, ballooning, canoeing and many others. Get in touch with specialists who already offer these services individually and come to an agreement on a commission package if you bring a certain number of people to an outing. Basically you market everyone's services under your banner and take a commission for doing this. Most of the time these experts will then also let you take part in the activities as well as an extra thank you for arranging the clients. That's how travel agents do it!

2. ARRANGE DAY TRIPS TO SPECIAL EVENTS

Do an Internet search in activities and things to do around your city or community where you live. You may be very surprised at how much is on offer. However, many people cannot attend these events due to restrictions on travel. They may not own a car, can't drive, be disabled, etc. If you are a good organiser; here is an opportunity to approach coach companies for a good deal and market the events as a special outing. If overnight accommodation is required, do a deal with a hotel so that you stay for free and get commission too. Most travel companies are doing exactly that! Why don't you do it to, but target a niche market and build a niche business for yourself?

3. AUDIO CD'S OF CONVENTIONS AND SEMINARS

The conference and event market is one of the biggest industries ever. Thousands of people daily attend seminars and events. However, many people cannot attend. So how about approaching the organisers of such public events and coming to an agreement where you can make audio recordings of the speeches and sell these via CDR or Internet downloads to those people that could not attend. Even if the organisers of the event want to do this themselves, you can still offer the recording service at a good fee. You would basically only need a good digital recorder, and a CD/DVD

4. BALLOON SCULPTURING

Don't laugh! I used to do this when I left school. Today there are many videos/books and balloon kits that teach you how to make balloon animals from these long balloons. It really isn't that difficult to learn. The hardest part is blowing up the balloons. That too can be solved by using a pump. Every child wants one. You can sell them at public events, fairs, flea markets and even busk them on the street. I also found that people felt sorry for you as it appears to be a hard job. Believe me, if you sell 200 – 300 in a day at a $1 each, that's not bad money for standing outside, having fun and entertaining people. They are sold in bags of 100 or more and you can make huge profits with this business.

5. BOUNCY CASTLES & PARTY GAMES

When bouncy castles first hit the scene, it was a closed market. Today one can readily buy them at fairly low cost. Included in this range of products are climbing walls, water slides and plenty of other fun items that kids will love at parties. Yes a small amount of capital is required. But think how many children's parties there are every weekend in your area? Within a month or two you could have recouped the costs of the equipment and smile all the way to the bank. Remember, everything one child has at his or her birthday, the neighbour's child wants as well! And hey, don't just concentrate on kids parties. There are many fair, events and even corporate functions where they will hire a bouncy castle for the adults.

6. CAR BOOT NURSERY

If you love plants and have green fingers, consider a car boot nursery. Basically you sell plants from your car boot! You will have to make sure you park your vehicle in a legal roadside stall area and then place signs at least 100 meters in either direction so that oncoming traffic has time to slow down and turn off to your stall. If you stand at a spot regularly, you'll build up a regular client base pretty quickly.

7. CARPET CLEANING

I recall that one could hire industrial carpet cleaners from the local supermarket. In recent years this has changed. For us it was such a convenient way to clean carpets. In fact right now we are looking for a company to do this for us. This business will take an investment into good machinery. However, if you look after and maintain it, you can reap the profits over and over again. Market in classifieds in the press and on the Internet. Do a mail drop at all the homes in your area and offer competitive prices. Don't forget to include restaurants, offices and hotels. This business than can build very fast if your service is tip top.

8. CATERING SERVICE

Many people (not just the rich) have private parties and do not want to be bothered with the catering. If you can offer a competitive price which is cheaper than them going to a restaurant, and do everything at the client's home – you could very soon have a booming business. You must enjoy the cooking and have good meals on offer, plus have all your own plates, cutlery, etc. Design your menus so that they offer value, yet are not too complex to make up. People will always eat and will always have parties. Offer good food at the right price and this could become a full-time business.

9. EXPERT WITNESS SERVICE

Have you ever watched a television court drama where an expert witness has been asked to testify in a case? Are you a specialist in a certain industry that could possibly be useful for lawyers in a court case? If yes, offer your services as an expert witness to attorney firms in your city.

You could also offer attorneys a service where you search for and identify expert witnesses for upcoming court cases. Here you simply charge a finder's fee. As the business grows you will build up a database and won't even be spending time looking for experts anymore. Who knows – you could then charge the experts and added commission for suggesting them to the law firms – almost like an entertainment agency!

10. FAIR ORGANISER

Every week when I page through my local free newspaper, I see a new fair being advertised. There is definitely a market for this and if you have good organisational talents and have an interest in a particular field, why bot get like minded people together and organise a fair that runs over a day or two. As organiser you can take a 10% cut, or charge a fee per exhibitor. This can be fun and once you build a reputation for hosting successful events, people may well approach you with all sorts of fairs.

11. FLOWERS AND CHOCOLATES DELIVERY SERVICE

I want to say that this is a simple business to start, and one for which there will always be a need. This is half true! You need some talent too! You need to be able to put together nice hampers and be creative. Start-up costs are minimal and advertising can be a mail drop and/or even a notice on your social media page. There are always people in love, anniversaries, birthdays and tons of other occasions where people want to show someone they care. It's not always about expensive gifts, sometimes it can be just a thought that counts. If you can come up with an inexpensive gift that makes people come to you - it's always easier to up-sell onto that. Best of all, you can run it from home, and you can make up gifts from anything. You don't necessarily have to use flowers and compete with the florists in your area. Chocolate can be combined with anything and will still make a great gift.

12. GARDEN SERVICE

A very good friend of mine was retrenched at the age of 50 from his company. Initially he was really stressed and worried about his future. A few months later he bought out a garden service company and today, two years later he has tripled the size of his business. He has 3 teams out on the road and enjoys a great outdoor job. A friendly personality with an efficient team can help you build a good business in a very short period of time. Besides mowing lawns, offer hedge trimming, pruning, edging and even weed control.

13. GUTTER CLEANING SERVICE

Gutter cleaning is a dirty job, but someone has to do it. If you don't mind heights and getting your hands and clothes dirty, this could be a good way to make extra cash. Most people don't think of cleaning their gutters, and then after the first winter rains, they panic and you may have to end up on a roof in the pouring rain. That's part of the job! If no one wants to do it – there is a market to earn extra cash. My neighbours kids play cricket and have often hit tennis balls onto our roof. Guess where they end up? And guess what happens during the first downpour in winter! I hate cleaning gutters, and I know my neighbours feel the same. Offering a service like this for a fair price can grow your business very quickly.

14. HOME SECURITY FIRM

I have a friend who started a security business ten years ago, literally from the back of his car. Today he has a huge premises and monitors 24/7 not only private, but commercial properties as well. Security is becoming more and more of an issue everywhere today. New houses are being build every day. Housing estates are more popular than ever. The Internet is full of DIY courses on installing alarm systems. Basic training is fairly easy to obtain.

Offer a fair priced service. Be courteous and professional. Advise the clients properly and offer a professional service. Stay up to date on developments and alarm systems. Service houses where you have done installations and keep clients informed on latest security developments. Word of mouth will do the rest.

15. HOME SHOPPING SERVICE

Everyone needs to eat! However, not everyone can get to a supermarket at all times. And it's not just your busy executive. There are the elderly, as well as house-bound people and those with disabilities. You will need good organisational skills to keep track of every clients needs. ALWAYS get your money upfront and get a few orders in before going to the supermarket. Work on 2 trips per day and make sure all the orders are in before the morning visit and then again the afternoon visit. This gives you time to deliver the items as well. To make this business viable you need a decent, but fair handling fee and the right number of clients to make it viable. When starting out – stay with the people in your area. As your reputation builds, you can increase the range that you cover.

16. HOUSE CLEANING

Who likes cleaning their house? Especially on weekends! All you you want to do is relax from the heavy week at work! Yes, you could offer to do this on your own, but what is even more profitable and which makes so much more sense, is to offer a house cleaning service where you hire out maids. You identify a number of reputable and trustworthy staff and drop them off in the morning and collect them agin in the afternoon. In this way you make sure that they are at the job. The more staff you have the more you earn. Pay them a fair salary and add a handling charge that covers your transport costs and puts profit in your pocket.

17. HOUSE CLEARING SERVICE

Believe it or not, this is a very in demand and much needed service. Not only do rent defaulters get thrown out of houses and these houses need to be cleared, elderly people and event deceased estates need houses cleared. From disposing of unwanted items to delivering furniture to auction houses. If you are fit, have a van and looking for a good side-line business, this could be it. Simply contact auction houses and estate agents and offer your service.

18. HOUSESITTING SERVICE

I have heard of this job and many people have spoken about using this service. If I was single, or starting out, I would think this to be the ideal job to have to make money, and get a roof over my head. I can't understand why more people don't do it. Basically there are many people, from business executives to frequent travellers that would rather have someone stay in, and look after their home while they are away, rather than leave it standing empty. Plus they pay people to do this! There are agencies that will find you such opportunities and they take a commission. Alternatively you can advertise your services on your own. You WILL need a very good CV and a number of references to prove your reliability and trustworthiness.

19. GARBAGE (WHEELIE) BIN CLEANING SERVICE

Using a small van, a mobile industrial pressure spray unit, plus suitable detergents, you could gradually build up a monthly round for cleaning household wheelie bins. The smell from some bins can be pretty disgusting. Not everyone cares to clean them themselves. A cleaning service is therefore useful, and a large, regular round means good profits.

20. INTERIOR DESIGN & DECORATION OF CHILDREN'S BEDROOMS & PLAYROOMS

Do you have children? Did you paint their rooms with fairy-tale figures when they were younger? We re-did our girls' room about 3 times, changing it each time they grew older. Granted, I have an artistic flair. However, so do many other people! Offer a service where you create a magical fairy tale atmosphere in a child's room by painting cartoon characters and figures on the walls. Have a few designs the parents and children can chose from and let the magic happen. If you create a special room for their child, they tell their friends and pretty soon all the parents in the area will be phoning you!

21. LANDSCAPE GARDENING

When I walk into any garden centre or nursery today, I want to completely redo my garden. There are so many new ideas and so many great things to put into one's garden, that I cannot see landscaping being as difficult as it was 10 years ago. Granted, you need a passion for gardening, a good knowledge of plants and a creative flair. Besides being outside, every successful garden completed is a promotion of your services. You will need the appropriate small truck to make it all happen. This is another one of those jobs that could become a big business in a very short period of time.

22. MAGIC SHOWS

Guess what, that's what I did as a teenager – magic shows at kids parties. It became my career as a young man and I worked in all the leading theatres, on cruise ships and even had many of my own prime-time TV series, because I started out as a children's party magician. Visit www.wolfgangriebe.com to learn a few cool tricks. Visit a magic shop and buy some fun props and offer your services in your surrounding suburbs. The focus should be on entertaining the children and you can also include games such as pass the parcel and musical chairs. In my life I have mentored a number of young magicians. Some of them do 5 – 10 parties a weekend!

23. MOBILE CAR VALETING SERVICE

This could keep you runoff your feet over a weekend. Without sounding sexist, especially if you have a bunch of pretty girls doing this (naturally supervised by a big man!) Seriously though, if you offered a 15 minute car valet service where you clean someone's car at their home. Have a team of 2 or 3 people and good cleaning materials. From the upholstery to the tires! Have a good strong vacuum with you as well. This is a service I have not really seen around much and believe that you could build up a big business in a short period of time. You could even offer a standby emergency cleaning service as well!

24. MOBILE DISCO

As a teenage I had my own disco. 3 Turntables and two tape decks! Today I see disco's run off iPods and laptops! How the world has changed. Yet one thing hasn't changed... people still need DJ's and still want to dance to cool music with great lights. The mobile disco market will always be around and if you know how to get a group onto a dance floor – you will always have work. Simply advertise in the classifieds and on the Internet. Decide on your niche age group and go out and have fun! Today projectors have become so cheap that you can even offer music video disco's! If your Internet is fast enough, you could literally stream right off YouTube!

25. MOBILE ENTERTAINMENT SERVICE FOR CHILDREN

From school holidays, to youth camps, to after hours; parents are always looking for ways to entertain their children. You could even create a club where the kids can become members and offer a number of services via this club. Depending on the age group this can range from puppet shows to video games and video game hire. Offer a value for money service and all the mothers in your area will naturally do all the marketing that you need!

26. MOBILE KARAOKE

I admit it... I can't sing. Even if I tried to sing at a karaoke function, I'm sure they'd throw me out! This must be one of the most popular youth and adult home activities ever. If you have a good quality mobile karaoke machine and offer a good selection of age specific music, there is no reason why you shouldn't be busy every night of the week. Again, just advertise in classifieds and on the Internet.

27. MOBILE LAUNDRY SERVICE

Who doesn't hate doing washing? I'll tell you who... the one that makes tons of money from it! Simply offer to collect dirty washing, wash it and deliver it back again, either on the same day or with 72 hours. Work on a realistic fee and get ready to employ people in a short space of time. This is very much in demand and a job that can be hugely successful in a densely populated area, especially a place where there are lots of apartments.

28. MOBILE DIAPER DELIVERY SERVICE

Most mothers with babies have a problem leaving home with the child. Here is a HUGE gap. Offer to do home deliveries and supply diapers at a reduced price. Find a diaper wholesaler for your supplies and work on a price lower than what they cost in the supermarket. Have a minimum quantity for delivery and advertise the service on your car as well. The great part of this job is that you can start it with you current car and don't need much capital. Once people know you are offering this service, you better have a good mobile phone car kit as your phone won't stop ringing.

29. MOBILE SNACK BAR

For years both my daughters did gymnastics. At every competition there were always two or three mobile snack bars and they always had a line of people in front of them. Whether you are selling sweets or toasted sandwiches; the sky is the limit. Get in with the right associations and be at the right events and this good be another HUGE cash business! Come up with a catchy name and start a franchise! The opportunities are endless. Find out all the health and safety regulations, get the appropriate municipal licenses and away you go!

30. PARTY DESIGN & ORGANISER

If you want to have an awesome party – phone me! That's one talent I have always had, I know just how to put together a party and which people to put at which tables. The right mixture of people is so important for a party to be successful. There are ways to cut costs, yet still create a magic bash that impresses everyone present. You could even build up your own stock and hire it out – from tables and chairs to themed decorations. I have extremely good mates who began a corporate events décor company. They sold it recently and had a number of warehouses, a huge staff compliment and a number of trucks, beside the millions worth of decorations. This is a job well suited for people who don't mind late nights and lots of travel.

Many people find it difficult to organise parties. There are professional party organisers who do this full time for companies. Usually they take a commission on everything they supply, including all services. If you can build up a stock of chairs, and décor; big money here too!

31. PERSONAL DINNER PREPARATION

Do you enjoy cooking? Many families just don't have the time to socialise and connect because of hectic schedules. Dinners have hence become a microwave meal that everyone can prepare at their own time. This results in dad eating in the study, mom in the lounge doing homework with her daughter, and the son eating later in front of his computer in his room. Talk about a dysfunctional family! This is were you come in. offer to prepare a home cooked meal at the family home, serve it to them and clean up afterwards. Basically you are the dinner chef for the evening meal.

You prepare everything and clean up. If gives the family time to connect and eat together. Focus on home cooked meals and start advertising the service in your area. The family supplies the venue, crockery, stove etc. You supply the ingredients and expertise. You may find that within a very short period you will have your week filled. Alternatively you could also prepare everything at your own home and serve it up at the clients home. In this way you may be able to do 2 homes a night!

32. PET FOOD DELIVERY SERVICE

Many people may have a need for this service, but your target market will be the elderly and disabled who cannot get to the supermarkets. Find a wholesaler of a good quality pet food and offer this at a fair price. Regular customers can keep you busy and it's a job you can initially start with a normal vehicle. As you grow, you can move onto a small van with company branding on the side.

33. PUPPET SHOWS

This is something that has died out over the years. And that's reason alone to get back into it. If I think back of my childhood, those were some of the coolest memories – going to the local library during school holidays and attending a puppet show! In fact my mom made me a small puppet theatre and I collected hand puppets. This is a fun business with a huge children's party market. Everything can fit into a normal car and you can even promote educational messages through the puppets.

34. REMOVE GRAFFITI

Someone has to do it! Why can't it be you? Find a supplier of good industrial cleaning material and advertise your services to local councils, and at homes where large boundary walls have been targets of graffiti artists. In fact a quick drive around you and surrounding neighbourhoods will quickly give you an indication of the potential of this business.

35. SANDWICH BUSINESS

This is an old idea, but it's been around for a while and many people have made lots of money with this. If you live in a city centre, or near a commercial area, many companies to not have canteens and staff need to purchase lunch or snacks in surrounding restaurants and take-a-way stores. Make a point of finding out all the health regulations, and start this business from home. Do some research and create a menu of a few select sandwiches. Drop these off at firms and stipulate that orders must be in before 10h00 to be delivered at 12h30. Now wait for the orders to come in and make your sandwiches. Deliver them in time, offer quality sandwiches and the business has to flourish.

36. SECOND HAND GOLF BALLS

Had you mentioned this business to me years ago I would have laughed at you. However today golf balls are really expensive. If you do live near a golf course and can snoop around looking for lost balls, or even scoop up the floor of the ponds with a net – you will make money. Clean the balls up and package them in 3's and sell them at the club again. You can even put up a notice and advertise in the club newsletter. You will be amazed at how much money people spend on golf.

37. SPIT BARBECUE HIRE SERVICE

There are many people who would like to host a barbecue, perhaps for a special occasion, or party. The majority don't always have the skills or equipment to do this. That's where you come along! There will be an initial outlay, but this is relatively low and can be recouped after your first few hires. Offer a combination of dishes and salads with the barbecue. Have a great tasting basting sauce with which to prepare the spit and away you go. As an extra you can also hire out crockery and cutlery. You could use a station wagon if you have a small spit barbecue, although a panel van is more suited to this business. Start by offering the service to some friends and if your food tastes good – word of mouth will get your name out there!

38. PERSONAL HOME HELP FOR THE ELDERLY AND DISABLED
In many G7 countries the local government will actually pay you to do this! Find out about it at your local council! Bottom line, the elderly and disabled need help with many chores – if you are willing to help, from cleaning the home, to assisting in personal hygiene, to cooking and ironing – the scope is huge. Work out a decent hourly rate and advertise in the local press and on the Internet.

39. PERSONAL KEEP FIT TRAINER
Are you a fitness nut? Have you done and attended fitness courses? Many people need someone to inspire and push them to do their daily exercise. A personal trainer is usually employed at an hourly rate at a gym by members. Alternatively you can offer an even more personal service by doing the training at people's homes. Your appointments will come through recommendations and networking in the right fitness centres. It is essential that you have the right qualifications and good communication skills.

40. PICTURE HIRE BUSINESS
Many companies actually lease the pictures in their offices! Can you source paintings at a cheap price? Maybe you are a painter. Build up a good collection of paintings and advertise them for hire to corporates and also anyone with a small business. Now offer to change them every 2 to 3 months with other paintings that will be suitable. From here it

could build to other furnishings as well. However it's easy to start with paintings as these you can transport in a new car. If you have old books and magazines, you can even create your own montages.

41. TIMESAVING SERVICE

Time has become a priceless commodity today. People just don't have the time to shop – hence the popularity of quick microwave meals. People don't even have the time to walk their dogs anymore!

Offer a service for which you charge by the hour and this can include anything and everything from washing dishes to walking the dog to buying groceries at the supermarket. Couple this with efficient service and great communication skills and you could become very popular very quickly. Target high paid professionals who are constantly on the move.

42. TRAVELING HAIRDRESSING SERVICE /NAIL STUDIO

Yes, it's always self indulgent to be spoilt at a posh nail or hair studio. But I would think it's even nicer to have someone come and do it in the comfort of your own home. This market is HUGE! Did I mention that it's a huge market? Think about it for one moment, who could benefit from such a service? Old age homes where the elderly cannot leave. Hospitals, Disabled people, other types of homes and not forgetting those ladies that just like you coming to them. You will need reliable transport and a portable make-up kit.

43. TRAVELING THEATRE GROUP

So you and your mates enjoy acting and have good ideas when it comes to putting plays, or shows together. Use your skills and market to public venues in your area, or create plays with social messages, or even corporate brand messages and advertise this to the relevant companies. Corporate entertainment has now become very popular, especially industrial theatre. Plus you have all the special interest days of the year such as valentine, Mother's and Father's day, Spring Day, etc; all allow for the possibility of creating show. From shopping malls to schools – a creative mind will soon build a booming business.

44. TRAVELING BARTENDER

To mix drinks is easy, most bargain book stores have tons of books on the subject at half price. Not to mention that this information is also freely available on the web. To learn the basics should not take long at all. Ideal for private functions and parties and you can use their bar, or design your own portable bar. If you enjoy parties and late nights; this is the home business for you!

45. TREE AND SHRUB PRUNING SERVICE

Most hardware stores sell hedge cutters and tools to trim trees, ivy, hedges etc. Many are not that expensive either and can be used to start up a tree and shrub pruning service. Start with small gardens and small jobs so that you can cut everything up and pack it in a refuse bag. Thus you don't need a truck, but can transport everything in the boot of your car. As you build the business you can look at small trucks and take it from there. Only once you have moved up in the game would I consider lawn mower and more serious tree cutters as that then requires a substantial investment.

46. USED CAR INSPECTION

Do you have mechanical skills? It costs money to take a car to the AA and have it checked out. Some used car dealers offer an inspection as part of the price, but these are RARE! No-one can really guarantee that a car will be 100%, but a good basic knowledge of mechanics and how cars work can prevent anyone from buying a dud. This is a service you can advertise in the cars for sale section of any 'private ads' on the

Internet, or even newspaper. Offer s fair price and work on anywhere between 30 – 60 minutes to test a car and do the important checks. Word of mouth and referrals will build your business.

47. VENDING MACHINES

I have seen these opportunities in Franchise magazines and some business opportunity publications. In fact I know a policeman who owns a vending machine that is situated in his police station. However, nobody knows it's his. Just on the soft drink turnover within that police station he makes a great bit of extra cash on the side. It is important that these machines are situated in places where they won't be vandalised and the clientele works gently with them. Thus offices, hospitals and similar places of work are safer to install them. Some companies will supply you the machines on lease with a small profit share. Make sure you understand the fine print if you consider this method of running the business. The power of this business is that you only have to restock the machine once per day or week, depending on where it is situated and how busy the area is. It works while you sleep – kind of the best business to have in my eyes!

48. WALKING ADVERTISING BOARD

Granted, this is not as popular as it used to be. But with a funky costume and a colourful board standing at a busy mall or intersection, many people will see the advert. If you happen to be a bit outgoing and still have fun with the passers by, it's actually a brilliant way to get a product or service known. The ideal situation would be to design your own board and approach companies to advertise for them.

49. WEDDING PLANNER

How much patience do you have? Good organisational skills isn't all that is needed. Often the whole family gets involved and arrangements change on an hourly basis! Thus besides the bride driving you crazy, you need nerves of steal to cope with the mother-in-law and all other relatives that want to give their inputs. Having said that - it is a HUGE industry and if you have the feeling for it, and are talented enough to make every wedding a success and get on with everyone involved, you could very well have a booming business in no time.

50. WINDOW CLEANING SERVICE

There are already larger companies cleaning windows on commercial buildings and sky-scrapers. However, there aren't many people doing this in residential areas. Many houses are double story and have hard to reach windows. Also, with today's hectic lifestyle, it's the last and least important job any homeowner wants to do. If you can work out a good price, or even a fair hourly rate and work clean and efficiently, there is a definite market here. Start by advertising your services in your suburb and let it build up from there.

> **Trying to be happy by accumulating possessions is like trying to satisfy hunger by taping sandwiches all over your body.**

YOUR OWN HOME BUSINESS SERVICES OUTSIDE THE HOME IDEAS

COMPUTERS, INTERNET & E-COMMERCE

One cannot even keep up with the speed at which Internet and technology is progressing. Daily, new opportunities arise via the computer and the internet. If you're in first, or just have a deeper understanding of how it all works; huge money can be made. It's all about communication, data storage, connectivity and don't forget social media!

1. ADVERTISING ANY PARTICULAR SPECIALIST NEED

Specialist groups or organisations may not have the time, skills or expertise to do this. Source people with these skill and offer these companies the people with the skill. Charge the specialist a once-off fee or charge the company a commission for doing this. Seek skills where everything can be sourced on the Internet.

2. ADVERTISING PROPERTIES IN YOUR REGION

No, not everyone is doing this yet, and there may well be a market to create a property website where you charge a standard flat fee to private advertisers, for a set period, to advertise their home for sale. It may be more difficult to get estate agents to advertise their properties, as they may already be on a bigger national site. As an up-sell offer to take interior and exterior photographs of the homes, plus videos! Never be dependent from any one agency and remain accessible to everyone in your area. Offer the same service to everyone and focus on the public and private seller. As soon as you partner with one agency, the rest won't want to deal with you.

3. AFFILIATE MARKETING

Are you one of those people that likes leaving comments and reviews about products, plus you have a large social network? Stop doing it for free! There are many companies and individuals that will gladly share a portion of their profits with you if you can persuade others to buy their product. If you already have a large following on Facebook, your website, or personal membership site, you will be amazed at how many people would pay to get exposure to your contacts. In fact some may even give you product too!

4. ARTISTIC PRINTS

Have you seen the projects done by design students on PhotoShop! Man I am getting old as I cannot believe the detail and dimensions they create on a computer. Anything is possible. You can even hand-paint a picture and scan it to digital, then tweak it some more on the computer. Couple this with a high quality laser printer and you can virtually print 'master' copies of your original artwork. Frame these is classy frames and sell them to anyone who is interested. You can even sell the pictures in digital form on the Internet.

5. APP DESIGNER

Today mobile apps are becoming essential for anyone that wants to build a brand. Smaller companies and start-ups don't have the money to employ a full-time designer – and this is where you come in with your skills and create the perfect app for them from the comfort of your own home! Here's the good news, even if you are not a techno geek, simply do a search on the Internet for simple app design software.

There are tons of video Tutorials on You Tube and plenty of apps and other tutorials available that take you from the basic right up to expert skills. It's not that difficult! Just like web designers initially were geeks and today you can create website with drag and drop software and free template software such as Joomla and Wordpress – the mobile phone app industry has gone exactly the same way.

6. BLOGGING FOR COMPANIES

Here's a sad reality for you! Unless you are an SEO genius, you will most probably make more money writing blogs for other companies, than trying to have your own blog and make money from this. Many big companies need people that can write about their products and do regular postings. They pay per post. You would need to have some writing experience and be able to forward an example of what you can do/have done. Start with searching online job boards and don't be picky in the beginning Build up a resume and experience and the bigger money will come later.

7. BUILD AND SELL COMPUTERS FOR PROFIT

Although this is nothing new, there are so many opportunities if you know what you are doing. I know people who simple fiddle with IT as a hobby and have enough bits and pieces laying in their garage to build up a number of systems. Most people are afraid to take a computer apart. For minimal money (if not for free) you can attend basic computer assembly courses.

Get your self a wholesale account and buy all the parts, put them together and sell the whole system for a profit. Personally Just looking at second hand computers is also a huge market, as nobody want to buy them. However a good computer tower to house the inside can often be bought cheaper as part of an entire 2nd hand computer and still be in great condition to house completely new and updated components.

8. BUY AND SELL COMPUTER BOOKS BY MAIL ORDER

Before I learnt about Amazon and online shopping I often walked into a book store looking for a 'How To' book on computer related topics. Whether it was how to build a website, or how to use specific software. I found it difficult to find a good selection of books, plus these books were always very highly priced. Hence there is a good market for good quality 2nd hand books dealing with computer topics. Advertise your offerings on the Internet or local newspapers.

9. BUY AND SELL INTERNET DOMAIN NAMES

I was surprised to see recently that .eu domains had just become available. There is still a huge domain market out there! Although .com domains are the most popular, every country has a different ending and some are suitable to certain industries. For example .tv is a great domain ending to sell to television and production companies. If you were part of that clever group of people who bought up popular .com names you no doubt made good money selling them again. However, this doesn't mean that all good names are gone. Also, people and companies forget to 'reregister' their names. During this period the name is available for sale. Big concerns will spend good money to get their domain back or buy a domain around their brand name. If you are a keen follower of the economy, you may notice a certain industry growing faster than others. Come up with various domain names, buy them in your name and then offer them at an inflated price to the industry. The options are limitless. You can even auction sites off on e-bay! To find out which domain names are available, simply do a search on google and there will be various sites where you can do this.

10. BUY AND SELL USED COMPUTERS

Many companies upgrade their computers, on average, every 2 years. These are sold off at rock bottom prices. Often you can resell them as is, at a profit. If you are nifty at repairing and upgrading computers, you can build up your own systems and sell these as second hand from left over parts. Simply contact big corporates indicating that you are looking for computers in lots of 5 or more. This enables you to get a better deal. I would also strongly suggest that you check each computer before buying them to make sure that they work! Once you have cleaned up and serviced the machines, offer them to schools, NGO's and similar organisations who would be looking for good deals.

11. COMPUTER PROGRAMMING

Just look at the popularity of downloadable apps today. Many people have made a fortune! Computer games are the rage! Do you have programming skills, such as Javascript and Html. Most probably by the time this book is in print their will be new ones added! Courses are available on the net and at colleges and universities. Some people are even self taught from books. The basic skills are not that difficult to learn and the opportunities are huge.

12. CONTENT WRITER

This is one of those jobs that never existed a few years ago. Today websites are springing up daily, and by the hundreds. All these site need good content. Do you have a knack of writing well and capturing people's attention? Can you easily research and come up with eye catching content? Can you meet deadlines? Many companies are looking for people that can write content for their websites. If you happen to be an expert in the product they are marketing – even better! You will have to identify companies that can make use of your services and market to them accordingly. It is a growing industry and if you represent a handful of companies – they could keep you busy for quite a while.

13. COPYRIGHT FREE MUSIC

As someone that owns a production company, I know the cost of music. If I shoot a commercial or corporate identity video for a company, it needs music. Most of the time this music has to be written for that specific production and takes up a lot of the budget. The musician has to create the music and then also sell off the rights to the company – hence the cost. Thus many production houses are constantly on the lookout for good quality royalty free music that they can openly use. If you are a talented musician and can string some jingles together and see them on on CD (or as Internet downloads) – you have a potential of earning a good extra income from this. Even if you learn to mess around with 'Garageband' on the apple Mac and learn to put together catchy tunes, someone may well buy this as royalty free music. Your target market will be amateur and wedding videographers, production houses, ad agencies and everyone in related industries that has a need for music. Visit http://ccmixter.org for a great variety of royalty free music.

14. CV SERVICE

We have billions of people in the workforce globally. ALL need a CV! Today there are many articles available on the Internet that will show you what to do. In fact there are even free downloadable templates where you merely add the relevant information, and 'viola' you have a CV. Formats may vary from country to country and company to company. However, once you have the basic information on file, it's merely a case of copying and pasting the old information into the new format.

Personally I feel that anyone should quite easily be able to design there own CV. However, reality is that most people today still think it is difficult to do. So take advantage of this! It shouldn't take you longer than a day to cotton on to the basic current formats needed today. Now you simply put out the word in your social circle that you offer a CV service, plus advertise in your local newspapers and on the Internet.

If you have a good laser printer, you can even offer to supply extra copies, anywhere from 10 to 100 extra copies at an additional cost. You will be amazed at how quickly these copies add a substantial amount to your profits.

15. DATA ENTRY JOBS

A search on the Internet will literally result in hundreds of companies offering you a minimal fee per data entry. Usually something like 30 – 50c per date entry form and some are even linked to a referral program. You will need a PayPal account or bank account in the US most of the time. Check out the various companies and chose carefully.

16. DESIGN A RANGE OF PERSONAL GREETINGS CARDS

In the early days of computers you needed to be a design guru if you wanted to create anything. Today there is so much open source design software available, including basic free apps from the app store that enable you to be a whizz at design. Couple this with Internet sites that allow free downloads of royalty free images, (http://www.clker.com/) and you can basically begin designing really cool cards. Buy a heavier stock card and with a good laser printer you have your own personal greeting card business.In the past you needed to be a PhotoShop guru. Today you can download so many free programs that make it so easy to design greeting cards and anything graphic. In fact there are sites that let you download copyright free drawings and pictures that you may use as well. Couple this with a good printer that can print on good quality card, and you have a greeting card business. Remember, you can design e-cards too!

17. DESIGN WEBSITES

This industry is changing daily? One change is that you no longer need to understand HTML. In fact today you can buy 'What you see is what you get" software. In other words, it's easy and similar to designing a document in Word. As easy at that! As technologies change, software seems to follow suit. I would suggest a good basic knowledge on how websites function and what search engines require to list a website on page one. Once you understand the basics, website design and building becomes quite easy. To most people this appears to be a impossible task. Like anything in life... once you understand the basics – it really becomes easy.

Today most hosts, and as part of the c-Panel include downloads of Wordpress, Joomla and Prestashop (e-commerce) that make life even easier. The only difficult part is to install them on your server! If you are a creative person – this is a great sideline business

18. E-COMMERCE - ONLINE STORE

Imagine owning a shop that is open 24/7/365! Yes it can be done and you can be in complete control with no employees! Who could have imagined this a few years ago? Plus your clients are the whole world at a minimal investment! If you can find something to share and give back to the client, this will also attract business. From a boutique store selling specialised items to e-learning courses; the sky is the limit!

Alternatively consider the Million Dollar Website. The page consisted of one million pixels (basically one page) and he sold each pixel for $1 to companies who would like their logo on this one page. Everyone wanted to see what the million dollar webpage looked like. It got millions of hits and all these companies got their logos viewed by all the visitors. I think the real winner was the guy who came up with the idea and pocketed the cool million! There is brilliant free open source software to create an e-commerce site – check out www.prestashop.com

19. GENEALOGY SERVICE

Most people are curious about their family history and would love to know who is part of their family tree. Maybe there was someone famous in the past that you were related to? The Internet is a hive of information and with the correct research (plus I believe there is software available today as well) you could do a comprehensive research for others and supply them with this information. You will be amazed at how many people want to know about their family history.

20. HOME BUYERS INFORMATION SERVICE

When people look at houses to buy or rent in your neighbourhood, do the estate agents tell them the truth with regard the 'real' conditions in that area, or are they just interested in making a sale. As in any profession, you will have your professionals, but there is always the small group that give the rest a bad name. In the property business, that small group does huge damage. However, this is where you come in and benefit form the mistrust that buyers have in agents. You supply them with objective real information about your area, and other areas that you have up to date information on.

It will take you a few days to piece together an informative E-Book/ pamphlet on everything in your neighbourhood, and this you can sell at a fee.

Many buyers will base their final decision on the information that you supply. Is the local school academically respected and does it have a good record? What is the crime like in this suburb? Do youngsters race cars down the streets at night? Does the local council look after the area and fix pot holes quickly? These and tons of other questions are important to anyone moving into a new area. Supply these answers for a reasonable rate, especially if you have a poplar large area that you cover. Market your services on the Internet and through various property associations.

21. INTERNET MARKETING SERVICES

Have you seen the term SEO? Have you wondered what it means? It refers to Search Engine Optimisation. In other words, optimising a website (whether company or private) that it is easily found in Internet searches and that it attracts a lots of viewers. Although this is a specialised field, I have seen many X & Y generation youngsters do this as if it's completely normal! For us Baby Boomers it's a bit of training and mind set adjustment. However, companies are employing people full-time to do this. If you take on a few select clients and offer to spend a certain amount of each time looking after their SEO needs, this can be a good money spinner. There is an interesting site called www.fiverr.com where people offer a range of weird and wonderful jobs they will do for US$5. I had one guy do an SEO report on my one website. It was comprehensive and ten times worth more to me than the $5. However, if I look at how the report was complied, it couldn't have taken him more than 10 minutes to do it. I just thought this was a clever angle.

22. INTERNET MEMBERSHIP SITE

This has become hugely popular today with entrepreneurs who have created sites with a limited high quality content of free stuff, and then a paid membership section where certain information for certain interest groups is updated regularly. If you have tons of relevant content and can offer a good return on value for members by updating the information offered regularly, if not daily – then this can turn into a big profit business.

23. LETTERHEAD DESIGN SERVICE

Today and decent word processing software, or design software such as PhotoShop or Corel Draw will enable you to design stunning letterheads. Couple this with a laser printer and you can start a small printing company! Find small companies and start-up business in your area and offer to design and print small quantities of their letterhead. With computers today it is so simple to save various designs, offer the client a choice via email and within 5 minutes start printing them. Most people have a computer and the necessary software already! If you are skilled at html – you can even design email footers as well.

24. MAKE BELIEVE ROMANCE

You wanted 'way-out' ideas – here's one. Today many single people are living in the fantasy world of games and romance novels and movies. Why not extent this fantasy with some realism? Whether the person is yearning for a romantic partner, or to be treated as a heroin in a story. Offer a letter writing service where you write personalised letters around the subject matter at heart, to these people. Charge a monthly/ annual fee and decide whether you want to follow the 'snail mail' (pst box) route or do everything on email. As your clients increase you keep track of letters so that you have topics and subject matter you can adapt and change for new clients. Try stay away from sleaze and keep it classy!

25. MULTI LEVEL MARKETING

As someone who has had much experience, and written a book on multi-level marketing, I tend to favour these business ideas as all the hard work has been done. Research, start-up costs and strategy have all been completed. Also, start-up costs are mostly very low and the training these companies give is mostly very good.

However, you must realise that any mlm companies rely's on numbers and turnover. If anyone advertises that you can sit on your butt and make money through them – look elsewhere. It is like any job! You need to spend a few hours a day and really work on getting leads and sales. Some people are awesome at this and make huge money in a very short space of time. But if you are not a networker, then stay away. You need to be self discipled and a leader who can manage teams well.

26. MUSICIANS - RECORD AND SELL YOUR OWN SONGS OVER THE INTERNET

Look at PSY from Korea with his song he shot for his fiancee, Gangnam Style! Within a few weeks it hit all records on YouTube. Just on 'Google Adsense' earnings alone he made a good sum of money. The days of 'sucking up' to record companies are long over. Have the right song and post it on You Tube. The masses will decide if they like it or not. Of course you need to send it to record labels and radio stations. But if the song goes viral, odds are you have so much more bargaining power and the agents will come knocking on your door! These days all hit songs have a music video on You Tube coupled to 'Ad Sense' and they all make an extra lump sum just from these earnings. Don't be shy to put your stuff out there – someone, somewhere will hear you if you have the right tune!

27. ONLINE AUCTIONS

Who hasn't heard of eBay?! Online auctions is a low cost business to start and can be done from the comfort of your own home. You may have a ton of stuff you want to sell around the home, or you may have a good contact to source items at cost. You may even be someone that buy's up job lots and batches of items at flea markets. If you have an eye for collectables and know where to source them, where better a place to sell them than on eBay. It's quick and easy and you remain in control. A great way to get into the e-commerce business and free to join and register. What are you waiting for?

28. ONLINE PROOF READER

Many print companies, corporate's and publishers need someone to proofread books and documents. Even authors and professional business people need various documents proofread.   Offer your services and set a fee per page.

29. ONLINE SURVEYS

One can get lost in time when one starts doing a search on the Internet. However, if you do a search on companies willing to pay you for your opinions, there are a number out there. Whether you are a student, home executive or retired, this is an opportunity for all. Maybe you have the Internet and software skills to set up a survey; you could even approach companies and offer to do the whole survey for them at a fee.

30. PRODUCE & SELL COURSES IN BASIC COMPUTER SKILLS

I was under the opinion that schools taught all the basic computer skills and that most graduates knew how to handle Excel and Word. Was I in for a surprise! Check out some of the on-line training sites and you will notice that Excel courses are some of the most popular out there! In fact any basic computer course, if presented well, will make you money. So how about designing on paper a correspondence course that teaches people step by step how to work certain software. You could print it in a few lessons and send out a lesson per week with self test modules so as to give students the time to understand and practice what they have learnt. This is suited for people who don't always have access to the Internet. And yes, there are many people like that on this earth; even today!

31. SPECIALITY REVIEWS

The entire customer service platform has changed since social media began. Give bad service and someone tweets about it as it is happening. Most countries have their own speciality sites dedicated to customer complaints where people can check the reputation of a company. Yet very few of these site are area specific. A market would be to approach businesses in your suburb or area and offer to do speciality reviews on their products and services. Design a clever site and market it to everyone in your area. By the time people start referring to your site as to the reputation of the lawyer, restaurant or supermarket in your area, people will start approaching you with their products for free, just to review them. As your site builds in popularity use adverts and affiliate links to create extra cash. Also, companies will start approaching you to come to them to review their products and services for which you charge a basic service fee.

32. TEACH PEOPLE HOW TO BUILD THEIR OWN COMPUTER

How old is your computer? If it's older than 2 years, try selling it! I doubt you will find any buyers. In fact you may have to pay someone to take it away. However, there is an upside to all of this. These old computers make idea 'trial models' to learn how to take apart and build a computer. I would suggest going on a course that teaches you about building computers (these are fairly short and inexpensive in order to gain the basic knowledge. Hey, you can also find tons of lessons for free on YouTube. Once you have the skill and are comfortable with how to dismantle a computer completely and build another up from spare parts; you can even offer this as an evening course to others. Advertise your course at computer stores, classifieds and on the Internet.

33. TEACH RETIRED PEOPLE BASIC COMPUTING SKILLS

At the time of writing this book, my dad was 78. He never used a computer in his life before. As I lived in another country, I wanted to stay in touch on Skype. The easiest computer to use was an iPad. I bought him one and today he surfs the Internet, send emails and Skype's me! Cool huh! At 78! However, many people cannot afford an iPad and may end up with an old Window computer – and that's a bit more difficult to learn. Either way, what about offering basic computer skill courses to old age homes! Now there's a market! Of course you can offer it to house-wives, students, older business people and basically anyone else. You will be surprised at how many people have extremely limited computer skills. Teaching them the basics – how to re-install software, how to install a printer, teaching them to understand how a basic computer works and where everything is stored. The sky is the limit! Teaching anyone not to be scared of technology and be comfortable with using it can be very rewarding.

34. TV SOAP OPERAS

Are you one of the millions of soap opera fans? Many people watch them, and many people are often most disappointed when they miss their favourite soap because of a traffic jam, appointment, etc. Some people would also like to watch certain soaps during the day, but cannot because of work commitments. If you have the time, then you can watch all the soaps during the day, and make a summary of what has happened. Type this out on your iPad/laptop as you watch, and then supply a monthly newsletter to subscribers, describing exactly what has happened in the past month on each of the soap operas. You would get subscribers from advertising this in popular woman's magazines and web pages. Be warned, you may need an extra TV and video recorder to video those soaps you cannot watch, or for the times that two soaps are on at the same time.

Yes, I know that most TV magazines and many sites offer discussion groups and give you teasers on upcoming shows. This idea is more of a personal newsletter with personal comments from you, and a more in-depth summary of what has happened. Making it personal will appeal to a certain target group. Not everyone likes off-the-shelf write-ups and reviews.

35. TYPING FROM HOME

Typing from home can be a very profitable business. Today most homes have one. You can download 'open source' word processing software for free and that is all you need to start your business. All your layouts, spell checking is easy to do once you understand the software. Advertising on local notice boards, at businesses, universities and colleges – people always need stuff typed. Busy executives could send you voice recordings they made on their mobile phones via email. You just listen to it and do a transcript. Easier as that. The possibilities are endless.

36. RENTED ACCOMMODATION

Just recently I had a friend who couldn't find rented accommodation. As house prices increase and loans are more difficult to come by, rental property is becoming increasingly popular. Couple this with students entering the job market, migrant families and business people moving into popular cities, the market for rental houses and apartments is becoming increasingly popular. Create a well SEO'd website where you charge landlords a fair nominal fee to market their properties. Focus on building a brand around the site so that everyone come to you, and you can start increasing the advertising fees.

37. RESEARCH AND REPORT SERVICES

Are you an experienced researcher? Gone are the days of sitting for hours in a library pouring through hundreds of books. The Internet has changed all of that! If you have the time and patience, there are many companies, institutions and government organisations that are willing to pay good money for research. Personalities and other professionals often need material, articles and books written by 'ghost authors'. If your command of english, or language of your country is good, and you can write-up a good report, then this is a good option. You can advertise on business websites, in business magazines and rely on word of mouth. Your fees should be worked out according to an hourly research rate.

38. SCHOLAR & STUDENT PROJECT RESEARCH SERVICE

Okay, not all students are lazy! There may be other reasons they need help with research! They may be holding down an extra job or two to pay back student loans, there may be a family crises that is demanding their attention, etc. Advertise at universities and colleges on the notice boards that you will do project research and charge an hourly rate. Once again word of mouth will spread the word for you. As you refine your research techniques and begin understanding the ins and outs of the word-wide web, this will become easier and you will become a boffin at research. This I would do as a business on it's own, rather than combine it with the general research and report services mentioned earlier. Although similar, both are different specialist fields. You will also find that the student market is not as high profile and the company market. But then again it won't be as stressful and demanding either.

39. SELL E-BOOKS WITH RESALE RIGHTS

I have created tons of Free and Paid E-Books – just check out www.mindpowerpublications.com. However, there are many sites, such as www.clickbank.com that allow you to sell other authors books and courses and receive a huge commission (up to 75% off the selling price) for doing this. There are also membership sites that sell PLR products where you can change the cover and add your name, and then sell the E-Book as yours. Simply do a search on PLR membership sites. Personally, if you only want to make money, I would go for the pure re-selling route and make commission, rather than the PLR route. You need good selling skills and an e-commerce site will help too.

40. SOCIAL MEDIA SUPPORT

At the time of this book going to press – social media marketing has become an 'in' job. Companies are employing staff full and part-time to look after their social media requirements. They need someone to make posts, comment on posts by followers and basically monitor everything, including the 'likes' and 'dislikes' on their social media pages. Today, if a customer has a bad experience, it ends up on social media sites immediately. Companies can suffer long term if there isn't someone that can react and try put out the fire. The market right now is huge and it is a job you can do from hope, or anywhere from your iPad or laptop! Charge fees based on hourly rates or amount of posts you do/react to.

41. SPARE PARTS FOR CARS WEBSITE

There was and always will be a huge demand for motor parts and accessories. Design a site that can find car parts in a few simple clicks. Obviously you need to know the industry and have a good knowledge of car parts and their prices. You could also specialise in a particular model and make of car. Finding a popular car model that has become part of everyday life in your city could prove a popular choice in spare parts. Sometimes prove more effective.

42. TRANSCRIPTION SERVICE

This can be for various industries, including legal transcriptions of court cases. Basically, anyone or any company that has a voice and/or video recording of anything, and need this transcribed into text. If you want to sit alone at home and not be bothered by traffic, co-workers and be your own boss – this is as close to the ideal job as you will get. You will need to get yourself a special foot pedal with which to stop the recording. To jump from typing to the pause button with your mouse while you type will become very frustrating – so you need a way to control the speed and stop the voice recordings to give you time to type.

43. TWEET MARKETER

Offer companies to tweet about their products and promote them online. Smaller companies are always on the lookout to promote their brand and create market awareness. Approach such companies and offer to do a certain number of tweets per day and on sites that you have subscribed to – in order to boost product awareness. You will of course have to be clever and make sure that people don't see you as a spam marketer. Creativity and clever mentions of products is what will make you successful and build a reputation so that companies begin approaching you.

44. VIRTUAL SECRETARY

Imagine being able to find a secretary on line to assist a busy executive with arranging meetings, typing memos, etc. You can chat via Skype and meet the client. You can sit in on Skype conference calls and type up minutes of the meeting. Your diary can be linked to the executive and everything updated regularly over the cloud. Today's technology makes this a simply and easy IT business available to everyone. Plus you could be offering this service world-wide. The market is absolutely huge and you could be earning money in different currencies. Don't forget all the global contacts you will be making as well.

45. VIRTUAL TECHNICAL SUPPORT

Are you a boffin in terms of IT. In other words do you know how to fix a computer and sort out problems? Many people can't afford a permanent IT person.If you can assist over the Internet, whether via Skype, on the phone or even written manuals – there is a large opportunity for helping the smaller companies out there. Simply charge a reasonable hourly rate for your advice and service.

46. VOICE OVER SPECIALIST & SERVICE

Isn't it awesome how technology has simplified many things in life. In the past a production studio cost you a fortune and you had to do a 3 year course to understand the basic technology. Today you can download free software and with a decent quality microphone, a nicely sound-proofed room, you can record stunning voice overs. These can then be email to the client without your ever leaving you house! Again, do research on some YouTube videos and you will be amazed at the potential for a great business.

47. WEBINARS & LIVE E-TUITION

Do you enjoy teaching your expertise to others? Webinars could be the answer. If you already have a large social network and people are interested in what you do, it's a matter of preparing your lecture and advertising it to your data base at a specified fee. If you are a teacher, or ex teacher and want to share your knowledge with others – have a look at TutorVista, e-tutor, Tutor and SmartThinking.com. They all offer school subjects with world class tutoring and you can do everything through them. Couple this with a few other video learning sites, some free e-books and as your reputation builds, you start building a following who will gladly pay you for your advice.

48. WORK FROM HOME FOR COMPANIES

I guess a search on the net for, 'Make money from Home' will result in hundreds of thousands of pages of results! Careful! Not all are legal and many are scams. Whichever company you decide on, do an Internet search on their background and credentials. In fact, just search for the company name, followed by the word, 'scam.' See what comes up!

Make sure it is realistic and that you can deliver the service they want. More and more companies are outsourcing work today, especially from people working at home who need flexible working hours due to family and other commitments.

49. WRITE SALES LETTERS

When I read some of these sales letter on website 'squeeze pages' I can believe that serious research went into these letters. Some people have the knack of writing a good sales letter. Are you one of them? You could ask really good money per letter. Companies, ad agencies, PR companies, Internet Entrepreneurs, etc all can make use of your services. A view well-placed Internet ads with examples could get you on your way to a big future business.

50. YOUR OWN INTERNET STORE RUN BY SOMEONE ELSE

Many companies allow you create your own e-commerce online store within minutes, and stocked with a great variety of products, plus equipped with credit card processing, order fulfilment and customer service. You simply get a cut, off everything sold, and it's up to you to market the site. Again, many companies advertise this for free – but check them out carefully before you get involved. Also make sure that all tax issues are sorted out and correct forms completed so that you don't pick up tax problems later on.

YOUR OWN INTERNET HOME BUSINESS IDEAS

PHOTO, VIDEO & AUDIO

If you are a baby boomer you will relate 100% when I say that this industry has changed phenomenally in the last 20 years. I recall doing everything manually, from developing photos in a dark room to splicing 8mm film! The digital age and computers has completely changed this industry. I still remember learning to edit Umatic video manually. Today it's become so fast and easy. 10 Years ago the price of a good camera was as much as a house. Today for under $1000 you have better quality than back then. The industry is even changing as I write this section.

What does this mean for you? Well, firstly it has become incredibly inexpensive to start a career in this industry, compared to a few years ago. Also, you can create product much quicker and with a much shorter learning curve than before. Maybe because I have been involved in this industry so long, I am biased towards it. However, I can honestly say that at no time has any industry been more exciting than this one. The opportunities are huge if you have a creative eye and are prepared to keep up to date with the technological advancements.

1. ACCIDENT PHOTOGRAPHER

Here's one subject under photography I would never have thought of. Recently I heard about this specialisation and basically you take photos of any vehicle accident scene. These photos can then be sold to the people involved, police or lawyers and then be used in a court of law to prove what really happened. As a child my dad always taught me to keep a camera in the car, and believe me, a photo saves the day! Most cell phones can take photos today, yet a professional who knows how the legal system and insurance companies work, can take the correct selection of photos and make a reasonable good living selling these photos. Start in your area where most accidents occur. Also, lawyers and insurance companies will start approaching you as you reputation builds. As you become popular and earn more money, consider investing in a police scanner to get to the scene quickly!

2. AERIAL PHOTOGRAPHS OF PEOPLES HOMES

Maybe you have a contact that flies a helicopter? At worst you can take a calculated risk and hire one for an hour. Find a suitable upmarket area and plan the route first. Now take a good digital camera or high professional HD video camera and take footage/photos of various houses. Print a sample picture with the wording 'Sample' across it and drop these into the post boxes offering the pictures for sale to the home owners. Don't just offer the picture, but options on framing as well as an offer to photograph the rest of the home. I know someone that did extremely well for himself following this route. Besides the work generated from this approach, he now had high income clients that phoned him for all their photographic needs, from special family events to company functions.

3. ARRANGE PHOTOGRAPHER/VIDEOGRAPHER NATURE TRIPS

Nature has always been the subject of art, photos and videos. Do you know of some awesome sights near your town or city? Offer tours and day trips where people can take photos and videos of the scenery. Learn some background information and history about the area and make this a special outing for all involved. You could even take photos of every one yourself, add this to previous photos you have made of the area and offer everyone a photo book of the day that you have printed at your local digital printer. This you then offer as an up-sell after the day.

4. AUDIO CD'S/MP3's/ DOWNLOADS BASED ON RELIGIOUS STORIES FOR CHILDREN

The sky is the limit! Most people complain they can never get ideas for stories. The Bible is full of them. So is the Koran! Years ago you needed to hire an expensive recording studio. today you can do this on a home computer. Research some great stories and then write-out the script. You can read them out yourself or get a cast of friends along to assist you. If you are part of a drama group, get them involved. I would strongly suggest an Apple Mac computer as even the desktop iMac as a built in microphone, and 'Garageband' software has loops, music and sound effects.

You can burn the stories onto an Audio CD, although the future is MP3 downloads so that people can buy on-line and download them to play on their mp3 players. If you are serious about this business I would suggest investing in a good professional microphone and looking at some good recording software.

5. AUDIO BOOKS

In some countries audio books are extremely popular, while in others not. I think it's those those have major traffic congestion, as people like to listen to them in the car. If you have a good voice, you good make these yourself. Alternatively find a young voice-over artist that is breaking into the field and who still works for a reasonable fee. Now record various topics onto audio. From How To guides, to complete books. There are many self published authors out there that would love to have their books on audio. It's a case of having a good sound proof recording studio (if you are in the industry you may already have one at the back of the house) and reading out book/message. Burn this onto a CD or memory stick and sell the hard copy. Or, ideally, upload the mp3 and sell it as a download off your Internet site.

Often one can even use the audio soundtrack from a DVD and simply sell this as an audio book. Maybe you know some speakers that have videos and who never thought of creating a pure audio version. With some basic computer software you can rip a DVD and create a mp3 or .wav file of the soundtrack. It's very little effort, yet you can charge a nice fee for this service.

6. AV FOR CONFERENCES AND EVENTS

As an inspirational speaker the one thing that never made sense to me in this industry was that we were the first to be 'cut' when the economy suffered a downturn. However, companies still had events and conferences even though they cut down on speakers and entertainers, they ALWAYS needed sound. The AV companies flourished! Did you study sound engineering, do you have a good sound rig. Offering to do the sound in terms of PA sound (Microphones for podiums and speakers) as well as background music is a bread and butter business in the industry. I know of two friends who entered the market and within two years they had huge premises and a number of trucks. There equipment was state of the art and they were/are worth millions. Many started with sound and then added PowerPoint, and video at a later stage. Simply market to the events organiser or HR/Marketing managers of big companies.

7. BABY PHOTOGRAPHY & VIDEOS

Do you have photos or a video of yourself as a baby, or as a child? Odds are you don't! Even though technology has become cheaper and it has become much easier to take and store videos and photos, people just don't have the time. In later years they regret this. Luckily I have my own production company and have always taken both photos and videos of my children. But even for me I had to make a concerted effort and put time aside. If you can offer this service at a regular fee and you schedule a 6 monthly or yearly visit – you will have a client for a good 12 – 18 years and can build up a booming business.

There is a knack to photographing and videoing babies. Make it cute and memorable. As they grown up you can dress kids in cartoon outfits, shoot them against a green screen and have them appear to float in the air or door superhero stuff. The more novel the videos and photos – the more your name will spread. This is a huge market that does not require much start up capital in the beginning. Even if you just take a camera that you already own, and just start with the baby pictures.

8. BOUDOIR PHOTOGRAPHY

This can also be termed erotic photography, but without the sleaze! There are many women, especially older women that would like to have sexy photos taken of themselves. Where do they go to? I have a photographer friend who has a gift with women. He makes them feel comfortable and knows how to bring our their sexiness, without them feeling threatened, or in any way exposed. Are you such a photographer? Someone that can make a woman feel comfortable and let her feel free to take personal photos for her partner. Do a search on the Internet and see the variety and style of Boudoir photographers out there. The market is huge and if you know how to make the ladies feel 100% comfortable – they will do all the marketing to their friends for you!

9. COFFEE TABLE BOOK

This is nothing new – however the big difference today with POD printing is that you can create a small limited number of these books for a reasonable price. I have seen photographic stores advertise the service in store. In fact if you own an Apple Mac, iPhoto (built in software) has a link to create your own photo books and order it from the software. They then deliver the coffee table book to your/or clients door. The great think is that you can even order one copy only; in fact that is what POD publishing is all about. You can even offer this (with a profit of course) to clients as an add-on service when you take photos.

10. CONVERT 16MM FILM, VHS TAPES & DVD'S TO DIGITAL

Many people still have old reels of 16mm film of the family. Even more have old VHS tapes and most still have collections of DVD's. Although Blue Ray is now becoming the norm, most people I know have media players and are downloading MPEG 4 formats off the Internet. In fact I have started converting everything onto digital format and found that an entire wall of DVD's can be stored on one hard drive! However, it takes time!

If you have the software and hardware to do this – it is a fairly good market. Converting old 8 & 16mm film is done by projecting it against a screen and filming that with a HD video camera. This is the easiest way to do it. VHS machines can be connected to the right computer video card via RCA and even firewire cables and captured digitally. DVD's can be ripped on a computer with programs such as Handbrake on Apple Mac and converted straight to MPEG4. Some research and a few trial runs and you could start a good sideline business.

11. CORPORATE EVENTS PHOTOGRAPHER

As a speaker/MC and entertainer in the corporate events industry I can clearly state that every function I have ever appeared at, has had a professional photographer present that was paid by the company to take photos of the event. Most companies want photos of the clients/ delegates as they arrive, during the event and also photos of any awards given out. Basically the photographer has free-reign to capture all the special moments and then of course all the main events on stage. Sometimes the companies even want special portrait photos taken at formal events which add a nice extra income stream to the fee. It's a specialist industry, but once you are in it, there is good money to be made. Contact the Marketing or HR managers of big companies to offer your services.

12. CORPORATE EVENTS VIDEOGRAPHER

Today corporate conferences have become major productions with intricate sets, celebrity MC's and huge budgets to create unforgettable events. Often a few hundred people are invited to attend these events and the people at the back cannot see what is happening on stage. Hence they need two to three live feed cameras capturing everything and projecting it onto screens either side of the stage and around the venue. It's a big video set-up and requires a good team of people who know what they are doing. Often the company will then also ask you to film and edit and corporate identity, or promo videos that will be shown at the event. Initial set-up costs are quite high, but the long-term returns once you have built up a name in the industry are huge. Again, advertise your services to the   Marketing or HR managers of big companies.

13. CORPORATE COMMUNICATIONS

Maybe it's because I have always worked with videos, photos and PowerPoint style presentations, but these are things that are easy for me to create. As a professional speaker I would dare suggest that 90% of the time I appear at conferences, the presentations used by speakers are not up to scratch. In fact I train speakers to speak and teach them how to create proper presentations. In the interim I noticed a huge market of this in companies and started approaching them as well. Today I have a strong sideline business where I pretty much develop their PowerPoint/Keynote presentations and offer video production as well. As someone that is reading this chapter on Video, Photo and Audio, I am assuming you are a creative type – hence this is another really profitable sideline business that can easily turn into a full time job. Offer to develop and design all training, conference and general presentations for companies. Create some examples of your work and market it accordingly. There are tons of sites on the Internet that offer beautiful free templates. Combine this with creative skills, some of your own pics and videos, and you have a unique product offering!

14. CREATE VIDEOS WITH TITLES FOR DEAF PEOPLE

This is a specialist market – but a big market at that. I have a number of Quick Tip inspirational videos I produce every month and post on You Tube. A number of deaf people have asked me to bring out versions with subtitles so that they can understand the message too. Granted, most Hollywood movies come out with subtitle options. However, many private people like myself, including companies and smaller film production firms have produced and will produce videos where they don't have the time to create a transcript and subtitles. If you have the necessary skills work on a cost per thousand words and either offer to edit these onto current videos, or even deliver an alpha channel video just with the subtitles.

15. CRIME SCENE PHOTOGRAPHER

It's not a job everyone wants to do, but you will always have work! Have you ever watched police detective TV series'? There is always someone taking photos of the crime scene. Yes many police departments have their own photographers, but many don't. You may have to do some training in terms of police policies etc, but that is worth it. As a freelancer you get paid by the hour, or per crime scene. Build up a professional reputation and don't get in the way of the detectives. Always make sure you take more photos than necessary so that you have covered every angle of the crime scene. Initially you will have to approach the police department in your area to ascertain what I required to become part of the team. Even if they have someone, let them keep your name on record for when their permanent photographer cannot be there. Do a great job and build it up from there.

16. CRUISE SHIP PHOTOGRAPHER

Have you ever been on a cruise ship before? What's the first thing that happens as you walk on board? Your photo is taken. The photographers are part of every event and happening, even on the land tours and every day thousands of photos are displayed for passengers to buy. If you are young, a keen photographer and want to see the world, plus get paid to do so – here is a brilliant opportunity. I used to work on cruise lines and made friends with a number of photographers. Many used this time and the exotic destinations to take their own photos and build up their own stock libraries! Depending on the country you live in, I recommend you do an Internet search on agencies that place photographers on cruise ships, or contact the cruise line's direct. In my experience these agencies have always been situated in London, Los Angeles and Miami. Most cruise lines offer flights, accommodation, meals, a basic salary plus commission.

17. DESIGN A VIDEO COURSE

Are you a specialist in a field, or have you found an easy way to do a certain task or skill? Visit www.udemy.com and check out their requirements for uploading a training course. Their standards are extremely high. I have a number of courses on this site and have made really good money with these. It is a great site, and you need to plan and shoot your course professionally. Once you are accepted as an instructor and your courses are uploaded – it runs in the background and you earn money while you sleep!

18. FILM CHILDREN'S PARTIES

We have all heard of wedding videos, but who videos children's parties, anniversaries, engagement parties, etc? Here is an untapped market and also special occasions worthy of being recorded and kept for years to come. If you are talented with a camera and know how to edit, why not offer this video service at these unique events. Find a friend whose child is having a birthday and begin here. As soon as the other mothers hear that you offer this service, word of mouth will do the rest. Naturally have some business cards, or flyers that you can hand out at the party too.

19. FILM SPECIAL SPORTS EVENTS

Consider the less popular sports and those where inter club competitions are taking place. In many instances there are 2-300 parents who all would love good footage of their children. Spend the day and record each event. Have a standard template opener and closer and work out a price per DVD/ memory stick. Come to an arrangement with the organisers of the event. As your reputation builds, many more sport association will approach you. Both my girls did gymnastics when they were younger and they had many different competitions per year. It was always the same photographers and videographers that were at these events.

20. FINAL MESSAGE VIDEOS

No this is not a weird business idea – there are many people out there that want to leave a final legacy and say what is on their mind before they die. These could be elderly people wanting to leave final thoughts for their children, or even a terminally sick person that wants to express their feels one last time in a dignified way for their spouse, children and family. Some people even want to leave their will and reasons for certain decisions on video. It is a specialised area of business and something you would market to attorney's, hospitals and old age homes. If you have an understanding personality and a creative flair with video, then this is a niche business.

21. FOOD PHOTOGRAPHY

Of all the photography subjects, this one may sound a bit odd, but everyone eats! Think about it, from restaurants, fast food chains, franchises, supermarkets to wholesalers in food all need photos of their product. Ever noticed that there are quite a number of food flyers in your weekly free newspaper? There are always flyers with specials on them in all supermarkets. There is a HUGE market for photos in this industry. Start practicing with food around the home. It's easy with digital photography today. Many photographers even use substitutes and 'fake' food for photos. In any industry, focusing on a 'niche' market is always good. This is a great niche market that can offer constant and big returns once you built a good name in the industry.

22. FRAMED PICTURES OF PRIVATE RESIDENCES AND PUBLIC HOUSES

As someone moves into a home, offer to take a photo and have this framed. In 5 or 10 years they can look back at how the house and surrounding area has changed. You can do large prints or a smaller collection of frames with the house at different angles. Simply use your imagination and come up with some stunning options for prospective home owners. With digital printing you can even create poster size prints of the house. The same can be done with corporate head office's commercial buildings and offices, especially on new builds. Be the first to offer them a 'record' keeping service of their property and sign a deal to photograph everything once per year.

23. FRAMED PHOTO SETS

As a photographer you should naturally have a creative flair. Consider for a moment topics or subjects where you could take a group of photos, whether it is two or more photos. Frame these either in one frame as a montage, or ideally create separate frames and show potential clients how one could display this on a wall in the home. One could even take one picture and divide it into two frames. The focus here should be on finding unique combinations of photos with frames and selling these to corporate companies for their offices, as well as home owners. Get journalists to review your work and give you write-ups in the press. Display your creations at fairs and exhibitions to build up your name.

24. GLAMOUR PHOTOGRAPHY

Firstly you need to build up a portfolio and you can do this by advertising at modelling agencies, in glamour and photo magazines. Don't restrict your self to studio shoots, but seek out popular location settings as well. Charge an appropriate fee to cover costs and make your profit. Once you have a good portfolio, continue marketing as before, but focus on the high profile modelling agencies and any location where up coming and top models hang out. Many companies advertise on the Internet and in local newspapers that they will shoot a portfolio at a special price and have their secretary schedule shoot on the half hour. In the end they have such a huge range of models that casting agencies even approach them for possible talent.

Of course all been fashion retailers also need glamour photographers for catalogue shoots. Once your name has been built in the industry, they may even approach you. If not – approach them with your portfolio and market yourself aggressively out there.

25. HIRE OUT A STUDIO TO PHOTOGRAPHERS

Do you have a large vacant area or room at your home or office? Ideally something that is at least a double garage size. Consider hiring this out to photographers at a daily, or even hourly rate. If you have some extra cash, invest in some lighting and backdrops. Backdrops are usually large rolls of white paper that can be torn off. A few colour lights against the white creates various effects. Visit a flea market and see if you can pick up some interesting props really cheaply. In cities space is prima and expensive to rent; thus this is quite a viable option and makes more money than a monthly rental to one person.

26. NOVELTY PHOTOGRAPHS

Here the sky is the limit, from dressing people up in Victorian outfits to Cowboy outfits. Add a filter such as a sepia tint and the photo looks old. With modern cameras and basic free computer software this is all possible. Think out of the box and take wacky photos. Add quotations or silly sayings and post them on the Internet to buy, or print them out and create postcards and greeting cards.

27. OFFER COURSES IN VIDEO FILMING AND EDITING TECHNIQUES

Over the years there has been an increase in post production video editing software and the market has changed rapidly. Ten years ago you had to mortgage your house to buy editing software that couldn't do what today's free software accomplishes. If you know the ropes and have been editing for a few years, why not offer courses on shooting and editing wedding videos, holiday videos and even short movies. With the advent of the Internet and You Tube, coupled with so much accessible software to edit, there is a huge new demand for this.

28. PET PHOTOGRAPHY

Here is a gold mine. We all love our pets. To take clear photos of people's pets in unique positions or doing fun stuff, framed in a cute picture frame always works well. What about creating a series of screen savers for the person to use on their computer? It's a good idea to retain the copyright and with the pet owner's permission use the best photos in montages and advertisements to get more business. Word of mouth and ads in local papers and notice boards at malls are a good place to start marketing you services.

29. PHOTOGRAPHY – GENERAL
Digital camera's have changed photography forever! You can even buy really cheap cameras today that give excellent quality photos. In fairness, you will need at least a 10 mega-pixel camera or higher if you want to charge for photos.

If you are a member at a club – maybe they need good quality member photos. If you have an eye for nature – take pictures and create calendars or post cards. If you travel you can shoot photos of everything around you and sell them as 'stock' photos with limited rights usage to magazines and web designers. The scope is HUGE and below are just some ideas of how big this market is:

30. PHOTO GLAZING ONTO PLATES
Anything from children, groups of people, landscapes, horses, pets and cars can be transferred onto plates or any ceramic items.

31. PHOTOS BY MAIL
Offer to touch up old photos – they can send you the originals by email. You can add special effects, frames, etc. You are only limited by your imagination.
32. PHOTOS OF TOURIST LOCATIONS & EVENTS
In the past you were limited to mounting the photos, framing them and selling them at tourist shops and at actual tourist spots flea market

style. Today you can create HQ downloadable pictures, calendars and books that people can instantly purchase off your website. If you do live in a city that is a popular tourist resort, you have everything at your doorstep to create a great extra income. Keep the copyright of your pictures and hire them/sell them to publications and agencies.

Does your city host major sporting events or even motor rallies? You could take photos and create a ll sorts of packages to sell afterwards and even market the next year event.

33. POEMS ON AUDIO/VIDEO
I don't know about you, but within my social circle I can immediately think of about 5 people that have written/tried to write poetry. If I approached them and offered to make a video or an audio CD with nice background music of their poems, at a reasonable price, I am guessing they would go for it. In fact a past partner of mine did that with video and managed to earn a nice sideline income from this. His price was very reasonable, but in exchange for the lower fee he asked for the rights to sell the poems on DVD.

There are enough sites that offer free stock video footage and music which is royalty free. Yes it will take time to search, collect and download the material, however, there are also sites you can purchase this from under various categories. If you are only going for sound, then subtle background music which adds to the mood of the poem is all you need. If it's a video, then the suitable titles and video background need to accompany the right music. All of this can be done fairly inexpensively and merely involves time and creativity on your part. People like seeing their 'own' creations come to life. If you can still negotiate rights to own the copyright outright plus sell everything for your own profits, you could build up a nice sideline business.

34. PRODUCE PHOTOGRAPHIC JIGSAWS OF ANY COOL PICTURES

You can take pictures of anything, have them mounted on a board and create a jig saw puzzle. These you can sell to stores, current clients and on the Internet.

35. PROMO VIDEOS & PHOTOS

Singers, entertainers, speakers and anyone that stands on a platform needs a promotional video. Production houses charge a lot of money for these. If you can create a basic 4 to 5 minute template where you just change the titles and simply drop in the appropriate footage on the editing timeline, you may be able to come in at an affordable price for the start-ups in this industry. The market is huge and there are enough people out there to market your service too. They also need good publicity photos for their promotional campaigns. You can offer a set number of photos for a special price.

A word of warning – many will not know what to do and waste your time as they are not prepared. So you have to treat them like school children and tell them exactly what to say, wear and do, so that you can shoot/ photograph them within a specific time period. You will have them a clear indication of what you need from them in order to offer your service at your special price. I mention this as I have a production company and once offered to do special promo shoots for a friend who started an agency. I gave clear instructions as to what the speakers had to say – but many didn't follow through and were insecure and unsure of themselves, resulting in longer shoots and more involved editing than I had planned. In the interim I have learnt to give clear instructions and direct 'newbies' clearly as to what they must do in order to get the video to the standard at which I am proud to put my name behind it.

36. PROPERTY WALK THROUGH VIDEOS FOR ESTATE AGENTS

The title says it all! Off to do a 'walk through' video of houses for sale for estate agencies. Work on a template so that the final edit goes relatively fast and have a standard order of rooms that you showcase in the video. Create one or two examples, using your own home, or even someone else's home and show this to estate agents in your area. Obviously the more creative and appealing your marketing video is, the quicker you will get the video jobs coming in.

37. ROYALTY FREE MUSIC FROM LOOPS

If you already work with video editing, you are fully aware of the cost and limited range of royalty free music. Even though some editing software comes with a selection of royalty free music – it's never enough. Visit a song writer or composer and you will be surprised at the high cost of customised music. If you are musically talented, great! You can write your own songs and jingles. Alternatively, there are tons of sites with free audio loops. Download a number of these and by combining various loops into jingles and songs and sell these as your own royalty free music to production companies and even radio stations.

38. STREAMING RADIO STATION

Internet radio stations are becoming more and more popular, especially for special interest groups. By combining Webinars you can even up your offering and have a unique service. The great thing is that you can keep a record of all your old sessions and either let listeners click on them to listen at their own convenience, or even sell the more popular broadcasts as downloads. How do you start? Simply connect your good quality mic to your computer and start a Skype session or sign up for an account with a Web-based streaming service (Justin.tv, or Ustream.tv, for example). It's as easy as that! Now go get the listeners!

39. TEACH PHOTOGRAPHY AT EVENING CLASS

Are you still a 'die hard' original photographer? The one with the darkroom and still shoots on film? Yes, digital photography has taken over and there is definitely a gap to teach people how to take pictures. However, many people are still interested in the real art of photography and would love to learn how to develop film and see their photos come to life in a darkroom. Also, offering this as an extra today makes the whole learned experience so much more insightful and fun.

40. TELEPHONE ANSWERING MESSAGES

There's a wide range to choose from, including famous lines from movies, humorous remarks, poetry and lots more. With a bit of imagination and a basic home computer with the right software you can very easily make many of your own unique messages and sell them to clients in an mp3 format via email or off your website as a download. Create a PayPal account and you are A for away!

41. THIS IS YOUR LIFE

I first saw this program on BBC where they surprise a celebrity by putting together a video and a photo album of this person's life. They usually also have a lot of friends and colleagues in the studio when they do this. Why not offer 'This is Your Life' video and Photo albums for couples to surprise their spouse with on birthdays. What about a 'This is Your Life' video/photo album when a child turns 21? How about a pet 'This is Your Life' Video/photo album? The sky is the limit!

42. TOURIST CD'S & DVD'S

If you are a skilled videographer and have all the equipment and software, a tourist video of where you stay is fairly easy to produce. However, you can create something similar with still photos by creating a presentation on PowerPoint or Keynote. Sell this as a download off a website and already you are in business. The latter option also allows you to add more blocks with information about photos and areas. If you have a creative flair, you can create wonderful tourist information products. On Keynote you can even convert the presentation instantly into a PDF. Many people prefer PDF downloads. The sky really is the limit.

43. TRAVEL PHOTOGRAPHY

A stock library is where professional photographers hire out their own original photos. In essence ad agencies, companies and basically anyone who needs a certain type of photo rents/buys the rights to use your photos. Therefore if you are a keen photographer and have a large categorised collection of pictures that you own – this is a good residual business to consider. Many people that work on cruise liners take photos of every country they visit and sell these to photo stock libraries, or even start their own stock libraries and sell their pictures to various magazines and ad agencies. Even if you take photos of traffic or people buildings in your city – these are all photos that are needed ever day.

44. VIDEO DATING SERVICE

The Internet has changed the way we do business in a huge way! Using free webpage building software out there such as WordPress, add some plug-ins and you can create a basic membership site for dating. Create a nice set and take videos of the people (at a fee of course) over and above the dating site's membership fee! Work out a good set of questions that shows the person's true character and who knows, maybe you too can become the next Internet dating site millionaire!

45. VIDEO PRODUCTION

In the 90's a decent broadcast quality video camera would cost in excess of $10 000. Today a chain store prosumer camera for under $1000 can shoot the same quality! How times have changed. However, I would still look at buying a decent quality camera that is at least of a semi-professional standard. However, you can already enter the market with a $750 and up video camera. Currently the requirement must be FULL High Definition. Do not be fooled by MPEG4 HD – this is not full HD. You need a full frame rate of 1920 x 1440. You will need a good tripod and some decent lighting. The initial set-up costs can be in the range of $1500 - $2000, but that's a huge saving compared to 15 years ago where a similar setup would have easily been 10 times the amount!

Many people judge a videographer by the size of their camera! You don't need a big camera to shoot a good video. You need a good eye for video and creativity. Also, stay away from hundreds of features on the camera. Loose features and go for video quality. The special effects can be done on the edit suite later. Again, Apple Mac's Final Cut Pro will handle everything. In fact their basic package in the operating system, iMovie is more than good enough when you are starting out.

I would suggest you attend and evening video course and learn the basics. Storage on discs is slowly dying out and most movies, courses can be downloaded via flash files of zipped movie files online. I have a number of courses on-line and this is the format I have followed. You advertise everything off your website. If you are shooting a production for a specific company/person or event – you can give them the final footage in any formats, from DVD to flash stick.

Create 'trailers' and post them on You Tube with links to your website where they can be bought.

Ideas of what to shoot and where to make money are ample. "How to" videos are really popular... here are a few:

D.I.Y. Promotional demo videos

Gardening techniques

How to become a better driver

How to become a video producer

How to use popular computer software

How to play (any sport here)

How to train a dog

Learn Stamp Collecting (or any other hobby)

Keep fit or martial arts technique

Produce sports technique analysis videos

Promo & music videos for new bands and solo artists

School plays and dance school competitions

'This is your life' videos

Train enthusiasts

Video record service for insurance purposes

46. VOICE OVER ARTIST

Weirdly enough, people associate voice over artists with someone that has a deep smooth radio voice. That is not always the case! Just as in acting, different products require different types of voices. The main thing is that you are not shy of a microphone and speak clearly. Record your own voice and market yourself to various companies that do radio ads. Video production companies often need voice over artists when shooting corporate videos that need a description of the action. The opportunities are out there and the money is really good.

47. WEBINARS

I know a number of people that are making good money from Webinars. These are basically live lectures with a selected group of subscribers who pay a certain amount to sign in and listen to you on their computer live. They can also make comments and ask questions by typing this in on their keyboard and you can then react immediately. If you have interesting information to share that others are prepared to pay money for – you can communicate to the world! There are a number of companies on the Internet that will do the whole set-up for you – most charge a reasonable fee. Here is one link that offers a totally free service: http://www.anymeeting.com/adw/Free-Webinar-Service.aspx

48. WEDDING PHOTOGRAPHER

Did you know that certain SLR camera's can now connect with an iPad via WiFi and while you are taking photos with the camera, they appear on the iPad and can be viewed? There the brides parents can views photos live while you are taking them at the reception, as an example. Gone are the days of printing the photos and waiting before delivery. With a laptop at hand you can place the pics into the bride and grooms hand straight after the wedding. Never has such service been possible. Not even a video production can do that, unless they have a live outside broadcast van, a huge staff and charge mega bucks! Are you creative, do you have an eye for taking great photos? Advertise at wedding venues and in the appropriate publications and build up your business from there!

49. WEDDING VIDEOS

Every bride wants a video of her wedding. Again a market with many people in it. Digital video cameras are becoming cheaper by the day and their quality increasing. Macintosh computers come with a brilliant basic edit suite as part of the operating software. Do a film course and advertise your services and away you go. Some wedding videographers are earning a fortune, and most of the work is on weekends, during your free time!

Create a template 'timeline' on your edit suite with preloaded 'Wedding Theme" footage so that you can simply change titles and place footage.

Today there are so many sites offering great opening effects, titles and short wedding theme videos that you can create an incredible 'Hollywood Style' production with very little effort. Deliver a 'magical product' and the bride will do the marketing for you.

50. YOU TUBE VIDEOS

Have you seen the number of hits that some You Tube videos get? If you create a You Tube account and allow them to play ads before your video starts (called Adsense) you are paid a small amount. It's something crazy like 1c per 1000 hit's. Nevertheless, if your video has millions of hits, as many do, suddenly you start making good money on You Tube! Do some research and see the topics that sell. Have some fun creating crazy videos and with luck you can make big money too!

Everything starts with ONE!
One step in a new direction can change your whole life!

When you start believing in yourself, the rest will follow naturally!

YOUR OWN PHOTO, VIDEO & AUDIO HOME BUSINESS IDEAS

TEACH YOUR SKILL TO OTHERS

You may have specialist knowledge that you can share with others and make extra income from private evening classes. Whether you are a musician, artist or skilled professional, the possibilities are endless. In most cases you will start with a small group of people and word of mouth will spread. Always offer a certificate at the end of the course in a frame. People will display these at home or in their offices and basically advertise your service ! Again, here are a few ideas to make you think.

1. AEROBICS INSTRUCTOR

You name the suburb, and there is a fitness class on the go somewhere. If you are a qualified fitness trainer, this is a great way to start a business that can build into a profitable venture for the future. Even if you start with 5 people in your own home and later on hire a local hall on an hourly basis. Start with a couple of friends and let them spread the word. You will be amazed at how quickly you can get people together.

2. ART CLASSES

One of my close friends is the only living artist whose artwork appears in the cultural museum in Frankfurt. He has taken to hosting evening art classes in his studio. He has 4 to 5 students at a time for 3 hours. They all have a great social evening out and often enjoy a bottle of wine amongst them, while the artists guides and teaches them how to become painters. Once a year they have a public display in an art gallery where they showcase and sell their creations. In the summer they also have an outdoor exhibition where they invite family and friends to come and learn to paint. My mates is doing really well with this – if you're an artists – why can't you do the same?

3. BRICKLAYING OR PAINTING AND DECORATING

Many educational institutions are always on the look-out for qualified people who can teach part-time or even in the evenings. However, there are also many people out there that are prepared to attend an 'informal' course, that teaches them the basics of bricklaying, carpentry, etc. This is a good opportunity for you to teach your skill to others. You could even offer weekend courses and advertise these in DIY magazines.

4. CAKE DECORATING

Baking is one thing, but to decorate a wedding or a party cake takes time and talent. If you have been doing this and have the knack and know all the ins and outs of good cake decorating, then this is a skill that many people will want to learn. A personally decorated cake takes time and costs money. This is a skill that will appeal to many people.

5. CAMERA PRESENCE

This is a skill you cannot learn online. In fact it only comes with experience. However, if you can take a lifetime's experience standing in front of a camera and create a short course for buddings actors and presenters, then this is a winner. I have literally had hundreds of TV appearances, many of my own prime-time TV series, so 'connecting' with a camera is second nature for me. As I have my own production company, I see how few senior executives can speak to a camera. 99% of people simply freeze up, even if it's only the two of us and the camera in a room. Often people end an interview and look up at the interviewer, rather than pause and hold that pose to camera. Why is this important? It gives the editor a few seconds more to create a clean dissolve or cut.

This you only learn once you have been involved in editing. Therefore, if you are a film & TV buff and know the ropes, advertise a course on camera skills for up and coming actors. Teach them your life lessons so that they enter the industry on a higher level than what you did. Offer course to companies for their senior staff that do interviews. Look at trainers that want to do training courses on videos. You market is huge.

6. CARPENTRY

In the olden days you became an apprentice to a carpenter (as well as many other practical professions). Over the years the master share tips and tricks with his student until the master eventually hands the apprentice their 'competency' papers to start their own business. I remember as a youngster learning carpentry from a friend of mine. In fact part of the learning curb was him allowing me to build a table wrong, and then make me re-do it. Boy was I upset at the time – but hey, I never forgot the lesson! Did you know that there is a way to hold a hammer so that you use minimal effort to knock a nail into a piece of wood? These are all tips and tricks only a skilled expert can teach you. Today both men and women have grown up in an IT dominated world. How many people have practical DIY skills. You can offer various courses – not just carpentry. You can include welding, plumbing, electrical and even painting. You may also be surprised at how many housewives would sign up for these courses!

7. DANCING

When my daughters where smaller, they attended numerous dance classes, from ballet to modern dancing. I was always amazed at the patience these instructors had, and at the same time did the maths and realised how much money they were making. If you have any dancing qualifications, it is extremely rewarding teaching children and there is a huge market out there. Initial problems may be to source a decent venue or hall. Once you have this sorted out it is a business that can grow very quickly.

8. DIVING

This is one sport/profession that you cannot learn alone. Safety plays a HUGE role and if you are an experienced diver, there are many people who would love to learn how to dive. If you have a pool at home, start in the pool with the basics before you move to the sea or lakes. Make sure you have all the safety angles covered and are insured for any eventuality. The first diving course I ever attended in the Caribbean, the person next to me drowned due to an allergic reaction to the air mixture. Who could have known! So be well aware of things that can go wrong. It's a great skill to share with others, as you are outdoors and keeping fit.

9. DOG TRAINING

My wife has a gift with animals. From cats, dogs to birds, we have them all. I am constantly amazed at how our pets play and react to my wife. The reality is, certain people have a gift with pets. Are you one of them? Maybe you even have expert knowledge built up over years on a certain breed of dog? Offer to train animals and owners once to twice a week. As the business builds up you can consider hiring a sports field where the training can take place. A hall is a good idea in the winter, but then make sure you have planned for those animals that will relieve themselves on the floor!

10. DRIVING SCHOOL

Different countries have different laws about this. In many countries you don't require much training to offer this service. Whereas in other countries you are required to do a course and become a qualified driving instructor, which isn't that expensive,. People will always need to learn how to drive. Be approachable and friendly, couple this with 'nerves of steal' and away you go! If you are a keen driver – do an advanced driving course and offer this training as well. Usually these courses are done at race tracks and offers to experienced drivers of all ages. My dad at 78 did an advanced driving course here in Germany and raved about it. It's not about driving fast, but about learning what to do in all sorts of situations on the road.

11. ENGLISH LANGUAGE SKILLS

It is amazing to see how many English tutoring adverts I see in foreign newspapers. I have even seen a number of them that don't require formal university qualifications. Many pay quite well. Often foreigners just want to learn the basics of a language so that they can communicate. There focus isn't on the rules, tenses and grammar. Hence the opportunity is there for anyone with a good school finish english to offer part time courses.

12. ETIQUETTE COURSES

How often have you heard the elderly comment that the people today just don't have manners, especially the children. When last has a man stood up hen you last entered the room, ladies? Start a finishing school for girls, and/or a simple general course in etiquette and manners aimed at men. Watch a few old movies and research etiquette on the internet. Couple this with your knowledge, add some adult life skills and create courses for young adults. Ou will be surprised at how many parents want their children have this knowledge. It's also an opportunity for well-mannered young people to meet other like-minded friends. You could even arrange special outings and build up a regular event. The only thing limiting you is your imagination.

13. ENTERTAINMENT

Are you an ex comedian, actor or magician? How about training other upcoming acts and either charging them a set fee per hour, or come to an agreement that you charge them a commission of every booking they get for the next 3 years while you remain their trainer. Many young people would be more than willing to do this to gain from a life-time experience of an old hand in the game. Simply put your name 'out there' and choose talented people to train

14. FLOWER ARRANGING

Okay, flower arranging was always something done by housewives and pensioners. I have news for you – this is not the case anymore today. In fact it is a sought after speciality and if you have an eye and experience in flower arranging, there are many people interested in learning more. Besides, you could even offer your unique arrangements for weddings and corporate functions.

15. FIGURE AND STILL LIFE PAINTING

Nude painting is always popular. (I wonder why?) But all types of figure drawings are an option. Still life such as fruits, ornaments, furniture, etc are also very popular. My mom used to do Bauernmalerei, and old German art form of flowers on cupboards and antiquing various items. Popular in the south of Germany! She picked it up from someone that offered home courses and within a few years was earning a substantial income from this, particularly from offering classes herself. This then led to further growth in porcelain painting, water colours etc. Today much of the artwork in my home is from a mother and a wonderful memory of who she was.

16. GUITAR LESSONS

As a kid I remember my parents sending me to guitar lessons. I can still play Kumba Ja and Rudolph the Red Nosed Reindeer! But that's it! Can you play the guitar? Do you have a sound knowledge of reading music and music composition? Guitar lessons can be done from your own home, are simple to set up and there are no real overheads. Any bigger city should have a a a demand for day and evening classes.

17. GYMNASTICS (RHYTHMIC & ARTISTIC)

Both my daughters did gymnastics from a young age and became national champions. Once they reached a certain level they too could teach and even go on courses to become judges as well. This applies to many sports – once you reach a certain level you can judge at competitions after some training. You may have a skill you didn't realise you could take further. What sports did you do as a child and how far did you get. Many of the competitions are extremely well-attended and there is always someone selling cookies, coffee and snacks at these events. They are making money too. The biggest problem was finding leotards for my daughters. Eventually one mother started importing them and another started making her own designs; they too make money. The sky is the limit!

18. HAM RADIO

Here's a hobby one doesn't hear much about, yet it's hugely popular and there are social clubs, magazines and of course the enthusiasts themselves. Normally one learns from other ham radio fans as they take you under their wing. If you are an enthusiast, nothing stops you from offering courses, creating your own club and also supplying the newcomers with ham radios. You can build up a small sideline business doing training on the subject and keeping stock of various ham radios for sale.

19. HOBBIES

You may have a hobby such as conjuring, juggling, or be good in acting. Basically whatever you are good at you can devise a course and offer part time evening classes and make good extra money with this. The sky is the limit here. I know many people that started this part time and now run full colleges!

20. HEALTHY EATING/LIVING

I have a wife who is allergic to preservatives! You may think, "So what?" In that case you have absolutely no clue as to the severity of my wife's situation. There are hardly any foods without preservatives in them. 99% of cold drinks contain preservatives, and bad ones at that. Never mind the high sugar content. The best thing you can do for your body is to stop drinking any fizzy cold drinks. And manufacturers become sneaky. They will put on the bottle that it contains no preservatives, yet they don't mention that it contains colourants and artificial flavour-ants! Many doctors today claim that most diseases today are the result of what we eat. Let's not even start with the fast food industry. Anyone in the know understands exactly where I am coming from. A few weeks of intense research will shock you as to what we put into our bodies! Inform yourself and share this information with groups or on a one to one basis, assisting people to become healthier by eating healthier. You could even offer public seminars and do keynote speeches for corporations on the subject. Healthy eating and living is a HUGE market today.

21. HOME COOKING

Don't laugh... this is a big one! Think about it, our youth has grown up with microwave meals. Anyone can prepare an amazing dinner today simply by purchasing pre-cooked meals that are either heated in a microwave or in the oven. Everything contains preservatives which aren't good for you, plus you don't know what ingredients have gone into that meal. Is it the good butter or a cheap margarine? Think back of your grandmother and even your mom's cooking. Wasn't that just the best? How about offering good basic home cooking classes for young ladies in your suburb. From using healthy fresh ingredients in meals to baking cookies! Depending on the size of your kitchen, you can offer classes for 3 to 4 young girls at a time.

22. HORSE RIDING

Many young girls want to learn to ride a horse, and even own one. Do you live on a farm? Do you have horses? Maybe you are already making money from this industry? Besides teaching people how to ride, there is also a market to help people overcome the fear of horses. Yes many people are scared of larger animals. One can do educational seminars on horses at schools and in this way also drum up students for riding lessons.

23. KNOTS

I was in the Navy and the first thing we learnt was how to make different kinds of knots, from a Reef Know to a Bowline – all part of seamanship. The bonus here is that besides teaching these knots and sailing skills to others, you can also create frames with knots in them. Get good white rope, make about 10 different knots and glue them on a board. Now add the names of every know and have the whole thing framed, These make great corporate gifts and are also super to hang in a bar. Go into any harbour area and look at that old Captain's shop in the alley; that's where you find such knot frames as well.

24. LANDSCAPE PAINTING OR PHOTOGRAPHY

Are you a creative type with good knowledge of painting, or photographic techniques? How about setting up a course teaching others how to paint or photograph landscapes like an expert? Besides formal indoor courses, you could even plan trips to touristy areas and other places of natural beauty. As the world awareness of our environment grows, this should become more and more popular with the newer generation – hence a possible great growing market.

25. LANGUAGES

I believe the best way to learn a language is to be thrown in the deep end in a foreign country where you have to learn fast in order to survive. This is the extreme approach. There is an easier way; personal tuition from a person who speaks the language. Courses on CD are great, but nothing beats live interaction with another person. You may have grown up with another language as your home language. Even if you had no formal grammar training at school, a language that you speak fluently is something you can share and teach others. You can either buy a basic language course book and follow a similar structure in your lessons. Or you can come up with your own approach and start with everyday phrases and pronunciation. Being German and living in an English speaking country, I made a point of speaking the language to my wife and daughters, starting with basic words and phrases and focusing on pronunciation; today they all understand and speak the language. Please understand that I am not knocking formal training institutions! But you as an individual may be searching for a sideline career and don't realise that your extra language can earn you money. Ask around and people will verify that it's so much easier to learn a language from someone who actually speaks it, than from a book or audio course. Today, Spanish, Cantonese and English are possibly the most important languages in the world.

26. MAKE UP AND BEAUTY

You need someone to practice on – this is not something you can just learn in a book. An experienced make-up artist can teach you the ropes and share tips and tricks from experience. I recently shot a promo video for a make-up artist and always thought eyebrows were plucked with a tweezers. She used thread and the technique is called, 'threading'. This is definitely something you can only learn from someone who does it. If you look at the popularity of make up artists and beauty salons, this is a great skill to share with others and you could easily build up a good business in a short period of time.

27. MENTOR

Whatever your field of expertise is, you may have made it to the top of that field and have many people that look up to you. How about offering a mentorship program where you guide and educate newcomers and startups. You can do this by offering courses to small groups of people, or even do it on a one to one basis. You need to work out a fair fee and maybe even a two to three year commission payable structure after your mentorship. Your fees can be high as you are offering specialist knowledge. I take myself as a professional speaker, I mentor upcoming speakers and carefully select only those students who I believe have a future in the industry. In that way I leave a legacy, and make an income on the side.

28. MONEY MATTERS

We all want more of it. Imagine being able to attend classes where someone teaches you exactly that! A no-brainer in my books! A friend of mine was always practical with money and had a good asset base at a young age. Her husband left her a while back, halving her assets in the process. Usually it's the other way around. However, this is what makes this lady novel. Now she's back on her feet and teaching other women about working with money and understanding investing. Needless to say, she is doing really well for herself. She keeps her teaching simple and fun so that anyone can understand how to save and make more money every month.

29. MOTORCYCLE RIDING LESSONS

All the motorcyclists I know, are very much over their bikes and always going on outings in groups. They tend to be over the top with their bikes and go on every possible course to keep them informed, safe and make them better motor cyclists. Are you one of those people? Then why not offer you experience as a course to other newbie motorcyclists out there?

30. PARACHUTING

Many people dream of doing a parachute jump, especially as it has been romanticised in action films over the years. Just look at the popularity of bungy jumping. If you are an experienced parachutist, there is a market for company team builds, personal training and adrenaline junkies. Work out a good rate per jump that covers the plane and all other costs. Be outgoing and make the students feel special – they will then come back for more and tell their friends about you!

31. PERSONAL COACH

Your speciality may be in ice-skating, rhythmic gymnastics, bowling, tennis or any other sport. You have the experience and knowledge. Many people will pay you to coach them personally and guide them to become proficient in their field. Your life experience can save them years of falling around and making mistakes. Later on you will see the heading, "Sports Instructor" and think that this is the same as a personal coach. No! There is a big difference! A sports instructor will coach groups of people. A personal coach takes one or two individuals under their wing and personally guides and grows them to attain greatness. This is much more personal. This individual is someone that sees talent in a student and walks the path with them, helping them reach their dreams.

32. PET GROOMING

I suppose if you lived in 'la la land' (Los Angeles) this would be a million dollar business. However I don't think many other cities are far off when you see the money people spend on pets. I have noticed a definite increase in 'doggy parlour' vans fetching and carrying animals. This is very much also an acquired skill with many 'insider' tips and tricks that is only learnt through experience. Offering courses for pet owner and teaching them how to groom their pet could be a rewarding and lucrative business. Take your skills and knowledge and compile a 6 part course teaching the basics, and then up sell your specialist services at the animal parlour, thus creating two revenue sources.

33. PIANO LESSONS

My youngest daughter is a pianist. Initially when she wanted to play I bought a cheap keyboard and looked up the basics on the internet. Two weeks later I couldn't keep up and had to find her a piano teacher. This lady even comes to her school for after school lessons. Even though I tamper with 'Garageband' on my Mac and can put jingles together, nothing beats the traditional piano. To be able to compose music, read notes and be so nimble with your fingers is just amazing. Besides it is also so beautiful to watch someone play piano. If you are a qualified pianist, the opportunities to teach are plentiful.

34. PUBLIC SPEAKING

They say that the second biggest fear humans have after death, is to stand on stage and speak in front of others. As a public speaker myself I see the huge opportunity of not only mentoring up and coming speakers, but teaching corporate executives how to speak on stage and be more confident in their presentations. This is a huge market if you have this skill and it is fairly easy to approach companies with a training course on speaking.

35. SAILING

You don't have to live near the sea, in inland lake will do as well. If you look at the popularity of kiteboarding and windsurfing, these are good starting points for people wanting to learn to sail. Plus it's an outdoor sport that will keep you fit too! It is recommended that you are properly qualified and have all the right insurances as well.

36. SELF-DEFENCE CLASSES

All those years of attending karate and judo classes as a kid can come in handy in later years. Have you achieved a high level of proficiency in self defence? Find a suitable venue in the suburbs and advertise classes at schools, libraries and shopping malls. Fathers and sons in particular enjoy taking these classes together. Today more and more women want to learn the skills to protect themselves. Both these markets are huge.

37. SEWING & DRESS MAKING

Once again this is one of those skills that cannot really be learnt from a book. You need an experienced dressmaker to show you the ropes, the tricks and shortcuts to creating beautiful dresses. There will be a certain process to follow and techniques that make your life easier; only an experienced and successful person in the industry can share this with you. Plus it is a skill that many people would like to learn, especially when you look at the price of designer clothes today.

38. SHOOTING: GUNS & ARCHERY

Shooting is something you need to learn from someone with experience. Not just with guns, but archery as well. You may have been doing this as a hobby on the side, and don't realise how big the 'hunting' market is. Living in Africa I have seen that half the people I talk to have all gone on hunting trips. These people all need to learn to shoot with a bow or a gun. If you have the skills, advertise on the Internet, in your local paper and offer shooting courses at a shooting range. Come to an agreement for preferential hourly rates at the range and add you profit, plus lesson cost.

39. SINGING

It is rare that you find someone that has a natural talent and knows how to sing. The majority of singers need training. Are you a singer? Have you had training? You can share these skills for profit. You will be surprised at how many people want to become famous singers. In most cities you can easily find half a dozen singing schools. Those that I know of also organise concerts with their students and even have the occasional singing competitions at local malls. This they do for publicity and to source new students. One ad in the local newspaper for up and coming singers should result in a good handful of students to start you off in this business.

40. SPORTS INSTRUCTOR

Both my daughters did gymnastics right up until grade 12 and both received their national colours. You may have done the same in golf, tennis, cricket, rugby, athletics, etc. How about coaching others as an instructor? Either start your own club or join an existing club as an instructor. It's fun, you stay fit and get paid for sharing your favourite sport skills with others. You can organise displays, host competitions and even become involved in national committees.

41. TAROT

Interest in the esoteric field is gaining tremendous popularity. Just have a look at the variety of Tarot cards available in shops today. Years ago they were tarot cards and you were restricted to one look. Today there are hundreds of new designs, from Fairy Tarot cards to Vampire Tarot cards. There wouldn't be such a demand if Tarot Card reading wasn't so popular. There are enough courses and books available on the subject. Master it and offer to teach others – believe me, in every neighbourhood there will be a number of people that want to be able to predict the future!

42. TYPING AND WORD PROCESSING

Even though word recognition software is improving at a rapid rate, there will always be a demand for typing and word processing skills. Besides teaching typing, one can also impart basic word processing skills on popular software. I am also led to believe that one can purchase courses from major software companies under license, and begin classes in that way.

43. UDEMY.COM

This isn't one idea, it's tons of ideas? Do you have ANY skill you can teach others? Udemy.com is an Internet site where you have instructors teaching you anything from magic tricks to memory skills to the basics on Excel. It is fairly easy to register as an instructor, but you will have to follow their strict guidelines in terms of course layout and your video and audio production will have to be of a very high quality. Within a month of posting some of my courses on the site I had hundreds of students and had already made quite a tidy amount of money. Today it is a regular income stream for me and I try add courses whenever possible.

44. WATER COLOUR PAINTING

Water colour painting can be done on so many materials, and can be taught to adults and children alike. If you are an artist and looking for a decent regular income, advertise classes in your community. You can even teach at schools and colleges and once your student numbers build up, hire your own venue.

45. WEBINARS & LIVE E-TUITION

If you like teaching and understand the concept of Webinars, plus (and this is very important) have a large database of clients and friends, then you can advertise a certain course/lecture at a specific time and date for people to sign up and pay a set amount, and then interact live with your Internet audience. I know a number of people that are making a substantial amount of money from Webinars! You can talk about any subject that is of interest to people out there, from scholars to adults. Some good sites that assist you with you with Webinars are: TutorVista, e-tutor, Tutor and SmartThinking.com. Couple this with other streaming sites, your own Blog, a few free E-Books and soon you could become an Internet guru with tons of people paying for your courses!

46. WEIGHT LOSS

If you want to be part of a billion dollar industry – this is it! Weight loss products and related services is a massive business. Maybe you have knowledge in this industry on what to eat and how to eat to lose weight. People need help and guidance. You could form a group in your neighbourhood similar to a Weight Watchers concept where you get people to talk and share experiences. You could guide them individually and as a group and motivate them to reach their ideal weight. The right atmosphere with a positive friendly attitude will make people want to belong to your group. We all know that the reality is that you have to change your eating habits and exercise. This is not that easy to do for many people – be there, help them and set goals and targets. If you have the knowledge, great – if not, spend time reading up on diets, correct eating, etc and inform yourself as to how the body digests food. Now go out and share this knowledge for a fee, but at the same time offer that personal guidance.

47. WINDSURFING

If you live at the coast and have lots of wind, you will have noticed the increase in popularity of windsurfing. This can be a lot of fun to teach others this awesome sport and as you build up the business, you could even offer to hire out wind surfers. You need not necessarily have a premises right on the beach, even doing this from your home one to two blocks down from the beach can work well.

48. WINE MAKING

Believe it or not, this is not as easy as reading up a recipe in a book. Living in a wine growing region I know a number of people in the industry, and this is not just an art, but requires passion as well. You could even teach students and up-sell your own DIY wine making kits and supply these to stores in your area.

49. WRESTLING

Have you noticed how huge wrestling as a sport has become? It's one of those sports you cannot learn on your own, nor can you learn it off the Internet. You have to be thrown on the floor and you have to know how to land. This is very much a one on one contact sport that can only be taught to you by someone that really knows and understand all aspects of wrestling. Many people claim it is a show. If it is, then you have to learn how to make a punch look wicked, yet it doesn't really hurt the opponent. You have to learn how to fall loudly, yet not breaking any bones or bruising. Do you have these skills? Many young boys would be very keen to learn wrestling. So what are you waiting for?

50. YOGA

Are you a yoga expert? This you can start from home and slowly build up the business. My wife who has always done yoga tells me that in order to remain supple and be able to still walk properly when you reach old age, yoga is imperative to keep the spine supple. If ever there was an incentive to start a yoga class, this is it!

Trying to be happy by accumulating possessions is like trying to satisfy hunger by taping sandwiches all over your body.

What you do every day matters more than what you do every once in a while.

YOUR OWN SKILLS FROM HOME BUSINESS IDEAS

TRANSPORT: CARS, BIKES & BICYCLES

Welcome to this series of mini books on 50 Home Business Ideas you can do with your bicycle, motor-bike or car! Yes, here are 50 ideas covering a wide range services you can offer around transport. I purposely did not just focus on ideas using cars, as I am sure there are some people who only have a bicycle or motor cycle and are desperate to find some way of making an extra income. So in essence, here they are and you can start some on you bike, and work up to having the flashy car, or bus in the future.

1. ADVANCED DRIVING TECHNIQUES SCHOOL

Many people really love driving – so why not put this into a career. Attend the necessary advanced driving courses offered and become qualified as an instructor for inexperienced drivers and people who want to improve their driving skills. My dad just went on a course like this at age 78! He found it amazing and spoke about it for weeks. Your target market is truly for all age groups! There are a variety of topics covers, from dealing with wet roads, skidding and even dealing with road rage. Also a great activity to offer big corporate clients as a team-building activity and have staff compete against each other.

2. ADVISORY SERVICE

Are you qualified as a mechanic, or just have really good mechanical skills? Why not offer your knowledge as a service to people looking to buy second hand cars. You could charge a basic fee to look at a car and offer your opinion on it's mechanical condition. You meet the people at the address, give the car a once over and offer the potential buyer your unbiased opinion based on what you can see/ascertain then and there. It's important that you cover yourself that the potential buyer cannot hold you responsible if there is a defect on the vehicle. Hence it is an 'advisory' service only. Most of us have no idea what goes on under the hood of a car. I am more than willing to pay a small fee to have a good mechanic come along and offer me his/her opinion. Odds are they'll pick up a blatant defect which I would never notice – that's all I want.

3. AUTO DELIVERY DRIVER

Some companies need good drivers to deliver cars throughout the country. Drivers need to have a clean track record and be safety conscious. Usually this is offered to celebrities, sports people or business people relocating. Here's your chance to deliver vehicles to the rich and famous! You obviously need a good personality, sober habits and be presentable. Companies then make arrangements for your return transport. Sometimes you merely need to deliver a vehicle within the same city, and on other occasions you may need to drive long distance to another part of the country as it is a unique one-off vehicle that requires special delivery. A bonus is that you get to drive some really unique cars and meet some really interesting people along the way. As this is a fairly specialised industry limited to 'specialist vehicles' you would need to be listed with a few exclusive dealers to keep regular assignments coming in.

4. AUTOMATIVE WRITER

Do you love cars and everything about them? Do you keep up to date with the latest developments? Approach newspapers and magazines and offer to write a weekly/monthly column on the latest happenings. You can attend events and launches. You can approach manufacturers and dealers to do reviews on cars. At times even lend you the car for a few days. The publications pay you a retainer and you get the perks of making contacts in the industry and riding some of the newest cars!

5. BICYCLE REPAIR AND SERVICE CENTRE

A bicycle is really easy to service and repair. Most people hate fixing punctures. If you offer a bicycle repair centre from home, you could very soon build this into a booming business. Start off with the kids in your neighbourhood. Advertise in local shops and at schools. This is something you can run out of your garage and you can have set prices for set services. As you build the business you can start selling bicycle accessories as well for an extra income. Eventually you can build it up to a booming business where you start supplying bicycles as well. Nothing more to it!

6. BICYCLE INSTRUCTOR

Here's something I have not seen around, and a business that could develop into something huge. Most parents (Dad's) teach their children to ride a bicycle, or else the children learn on their own. The question is, how much skill do they really have on that bicycle? Do they understand the safety issues, road rules, etc? How about offering a driving instruction school for bicycles? How many parents are divorced today and don't have time to teach their children the basics of a bicycle, but still require their kids to cycle to school? This is a huge target market where for a reasonable fee you offer to train children in the correct and safe ways of riding a bicycle. You could come up with a basic 3 week course with 2 lessons a week. Have a starter bike with safety wheels for youngsters. Most people don't buy the correct size bicycles for their kids. Offer to source and supply the right size bicycle as an added income. Approach kindergartens and schools and offer courses right there! This can become a huge business!

7. BICYCLE TAXI

I saw this for the first time in Hamburg, Germany and it's a brilliant idea. Someone took three wheeler bicycles and added a two seater canopy at the back. These bicycles ride throughout the city centre and for the fraction of a taxi price, they take people too and fro throughout the city. As it has a canopy, they can ride in the rain. The 'driver' stays fit as it is all pedal power. The owner simply rent's the bikes out to youngsters who want to earn extra cash, and that's how he makes money. You can look it up on the Internet and I am sure other cities have slowly started to follow suit.

8. BUY & SELL BICYCLES

Anything that involves buying and selling requires some start-up capital. However, you may have some old bicycles in your garage. I just cleaned out my garage and as I have 2 daughters, found 4 old bicycles gathering dust. I spent a morning cleaning them up and making sure everything works and advertised them on the Internet. Within a day I had sold all four and had extra cash in my hand. I figured, with this I could go look for other old bicycles, fix and clean them and sell these too. Hence I personally feel that start up capital shouldn't be such an issue here, as most of us (even if we don't have old bicycles) have some junk in the garage or home we can sell to get initial start-up money in. Granted, you are not going to make hundreds of dollars per sale, but within a month you may well have made enough money to start expanding, or even progress to buying motor cycles.

9. BUY & SELL MOTOR CARS

You could have built up your bicycle or motor cycle business and made enough start-up money to progress to cars. You can even start with just one car! You may even have an old car in the back yard. If you have mechanical knowledge and interest in cars, this can be a fun business.

You could even raise starting capital buy selling your current car for a profit, and using that to buy the first car that you then sell again for profit, and so on. You would need to look in the local classifieds, on the Internet and be a clever business person. Remember, the profit you make is not only when you sell, but more importantly when you buy. Buy at a good price and ideally a car that doesn't need much or any work on it, and then sell at a good profit.

10. CAR DEALERSHIPS PART TIME SALES

When last have you walked into a car dealership and been blown away by awesome passionate service? Odds are... never! Are you passionate about a certain brand of car? Approach the dealership in your area and offer to come in part-time on Saturday mornings. Odds are your passion will become infectious and draw potential customers to you. You could end up selling way more cars that the permanent staff. As you do it only on Saturdays, you are not really a threat to the permanent staff and they can take time off while you go and enjoy your passion. You can work on a basic hourly rate. However, if you have what it takes, the dealership will be way more open to offering you a commission per car you sell. If the passion is there that's the way you should go!

11. CAR WASH

It has become really expensive to wash cars. Couple this with certain countries that have environmental laws and it becomes a problem. If you can do this in your front garden with the family over weekends at a fair price; there may be a market in your neighbourhood. If you are more progressive in your thinking and a pretty girl, or a group of pretty girls washing cars in bikini's will always be a good bet, regardless of whether you see this as sexist or not.

12. CHAUFFEUR SERVICE

You have two options here.

a.) You may own a prestige motor car and can offer it out for hire and chauffeur drive it yourself. From dinner dates, school balls, company events; the opportunities are endless.

b.) You may have time in the day and good driving skills. Thus you can offer to become the driver/chauffeur for wealthy people who have lost their driving license, have no driving experience, or just need someone to drive them around due to their busy schedule. Have your own smart uniform and offer your services at an hourly or daily rate.

13. CHAUFFEURING SERVICE FOR DISABLED PEOPLE

This is very different to the above example, as here you are not driving an expensive car for wealthy people/business people, but most probably driving a mini van/bus which has been fitted with wheelchair rear hydraulic life and suitable seating for disables people. Alternatively you can also concentrate on the elderly. These people struggle to find reliable transport and are always in need of this service. Build up a reliable, caring reputation and you could very soon have a booming business. However, be aware of the laws of your country and make sure you have the correct license and insurances for your vehicle.

14. CLASSIC CAR HIRE BUSINESS

If you have mechanical knowledge and can fix old cars; major bonus! I know many collectors of classic cars that have gone into this business. Think about it, any new sports car costs a fortune. However, and old timer redone up and fixed to mint condition will usually cost you far less, yet appears as prestige as that latest model expensive sports car. At a traffic light, odds are people will look at the old timer first. I have often seen 20-year old classics as well as sports cars that are as, if not more impressive, than the new cars. Just think of the old 'Knight-rider' series with the 'Kit' car. Imagine finding an old Pontiac, restoring it and hiring it out as that; would be appealing to most of the 'baby-boomer' generation.

15. CLUB CO-ORDINATOR

Start a bicycle, motor cycle or car club! It's your club and you run it! From a mountain biking club every Sunday for bicycle enthusiasts, to a motor cycle long distance off road club to a classic car club. You source all the relevant interested parties and become the founding member of the club/association. You need to make the club appealing with regular events. Your membership fees bring in a regular income. The more creative and active you are in drawing interested members, the more you earn.

16. COURIER BUSINESS USING YOUR VAN TO DELIVER PARCELS

This is also big business and a competitive market for the established firms offering this service. If you come in and offer quick deliveries with maybe 100km radius for companies that need extra help on specific days. You will be surprised at how quickly you can become extremely busy.

17. CUSTOM CAR DESIGNS

Are you artistic? How about offering to do custom paint jobs/designs on cars. This is a specialised market and you would not necessarily have to do everything with spray paint, although this would be preferred. However, you can also hand paint certain designs and logos to customer specifications.

18. DELIVER CARS FOR MONEY

One often thinks that car dealers only have the cars delivered by the head office, or supplier. However, they often buy cars from auctions and private deals and do need someone to drive the car to their showroom. Private business people who fly often don't want to leave their cars at the airport, and look for people to drive their cars back home. You obviously need a valid driver's license and also an insurance that covers you in these vehicles.

19. DELIVERY DRIVERS FOR FAST FOOD CHAINS

I have often had fast food delivered to my home by someone on a scooter or small car. Most of these outlets offer home delivery and hire people on a part time basis. So whether you have a scooter or reliable vehicle, this is a market one can look at. These companies usually have magnetic signage that you simply stick to the side of your car, or roof racks with their signage on. It can easily be added or removed to your vehicle. The bonus is that you may even earn tips at the deliveries.

20. DELIVERY SERVICE FOR FOOD SHOPS TO CUSTOMERS

Most big supermarkets are offering a home delivery service and most are tender applications and difficult to land. However, it's not impossible if the tender opens up and you apply in time. There are also smaller shops (and this is your starting target market) from gift shops, pharmacies, furniture stores, Delhi's etc.that would also like to offer this service, but cannot afford a full time driver. Work out a delivery cost in relation to distance driven and offer this to these stores. Very soon you could be very busy delivering goods throughout your neighbourhood.

21. DENT REMOVAL

Just visit You Tube and do a search on 'Dent removal'. There are tons of videos that show you how easy it is, even 'paint-less' dent removal. You may have experience in this field which makes it even easier. Many dents are minor and not worth the time and money to take the vehicle in to have them repaired. Imagine offering a home dent removal service where you can fix dents within a few minutes and charge a fair call-out rate. Advertise this in the local newspaper and even at the local garage. Even if you know nothing about dent removal and start researching this from scratch. The basic tools are not going to cost you much and it's a great sideline business over weekends.

22. DRIVING INSTRUCTOR

If you enjoy people and enjoy driving, why not teach people to drive. Yes, initially it is an outlay to buy a vehicle with dual controls. However, I have seen many driving instructors use normal vehicles. I would assume this is dependent on the country you live in. I assume it can be stressful at times. However, you can always start teaching at an established driving school and learn the ropes from them in terms of keeping it safe and simple. Obviously you would again need the right license and insurances.

23. DRIVER RECRUITMENT AGENT

Whether it's a company looking for long haul drivers, or fast food shops looking for delivery drivers, you could begin a company that sources drivers for various industries – almost like a recruitment agent specialising in drivers. If you have an interest in the industry, you will soon know what the requirements are for long haul drivers versus, school bus drivers. You could have categories from hearse drivers to armoUred car drivers. Collect CV's and references and offer to source drivers for various companies at a fee.

24. ERRAND SERVICES

This is a simple business to start for virtually no money at all. You can even do it if you have a car, motor cycle or bicycle! Basically we all have busy life styles and people don't have time for the 'little' things such as returning a library book or DVD; picking up groceries for a busy professional, or just dropping off a child's lunch box at school that they forgot at home. The sky is the limit. You would need a mobile phone and let everyone in your suburb know that you are available to do small errands at a moments notice. Obviously the busier you get, you may need a team of people on the road. The success of this business is in having personal contact and trust with your clients as well as a good knowledge of everything available in your area that you are working in. As you become known, even the people to whom you have delivered goods will start utilising your service. It's a business that will market itself.

25. FURNITURE REMOVAL

This is big business! Do yourself a favoUr... phone around and get a quote from various companies to have a dining room table and chairs delivered. You will be surprised at what people charge for this service. Furthermore, I don't think you will get anyone to do this on the same day you phone them. Most people are booked up for days in advance. A good quality 2nd hand truck, or even these new cheap far east imports are great value for money. You would need someone to help you carry the furniture and someone at home to take the inquiries. Alternatively, have a phone car kit which the assistant can answer while out on deliveries and add new jobs in the diary.

26. FITTING OF DVD/ENTERTAINMENT SYSTEMS

Basic understanding of car electronics is required here. One can gain experience at the vehicle fitment centre over a few weekends to see how one fits these radio & entertainment systems. Again, people don't have the time to book their vehicles in and wait for this service. If you have the experience and can offer competitive rates, then you can offer to do this at people's homes. Find a supplier that will give you a good deal on basic range of systems. Have pictures and stats of these that you can advertise on a website or send out in an email. Don't have a large choice – keep it basic and look for systems that are easy to install. I don't see people offering this as a home installation service. With the right price and good marketing at some local stores in your area, this could start as a weekend job and very soon become a booming business.

27. LUNCH DELIVERY SERVICE

Combine your culinary skills with transport! Deliver sandwiches to companies. If you have a commercial office complex or area near you, put out some flyers that you offer fresh sandwiches delivered to the offices. Have a set selection and time by which the order must be placed, and then deliver them. I know a few people that started this quietly on the side and now have a booming business.

28. MARKETING MATERIAL DISTRIBUTION

If you have a small van or station wagon, many companies and even newspapers are in need of a door to door delivery service. This usually involves carry a stock of a few thousand pamphlets in the back of the vehicle and having one or two runners putting the items into post boxes in residential areas. You simply drive very slowly giving your runners a chance to deliver all the marketing material. It is usually also limited to one or two suburbs per day. You can approach newspapers, magazines and big companies.

29. MESSENGER SERVICE

This is very similar to a courier service, except here you don't need a van, but can use a normal sedan. Here, you would be required to deliver 'sensitive' documents and letters, i.e. confidential documents. You would most probably have to sign some form of confidentiality agreement with the companies involved, acknowledging that you will not divulge anything about the documents you handle. It's a niche market, but can be very lucrative if you break into it.

30. MOBILE ADVERTISING VEHICLE

If you have a trailer in the drive-way collecting dust, it doesn't take much to weld an 'A-Frame' with large boards on the side onto it and offer to advertise anything for companies. You then work out a cost per hour rate to drive through certain busy areas and expose the product/ brand to people seeing you drive by. This is very popular over weekends at sports events or at the beach. You could even stick magnetic signage on the side of your car. Work out a good deal with a signage maker so that when the client has these signs made up (obviously at their costs) that you get a percentage commission back on every job you refer to the signage maker; that's an extra income for you on the side!

31. MODEL COLLECTOR/BUILDER

I know of a number of people who not only collect, but also build model cars, as well as motor cycles. This has become a huge business and there are some very high priced models out there. Most collectors belong to associations and these models are traded, bought and sold amongst members. As in any hobby, there are some people that take this seriously and make a good sideline income building, sourcing and selling these models to other hobbyists. If this is something that interests you – it's a great sideline business to start from home.

32. MOTOR CYCLE DESIGNER

Have you ever watched that program on discovery with the guys that built these custom bikes? It's amazing what they do! Do you have a mechanical or engineering background and a love for motor cycles. Many people love coming up with their own bike designs. Compared to a motor car where a custom build will cost a fortune, it is far less expensive to build a custom bike. You may already have a few spare parts and be repairing motor cycles on the side. With a bit of creative imagination and solid mechanical knowledge, you may just be able to piece together a unique looking bike and sell it at a good profit. Take photos of each bike you sell and start advertising your custom designs. Remember, Rome wasn't built in a day! Start small and you never know, soon Discovery may commission a series on your success story!

33. NEWSPAPER DELIVERY SERVICE

This is ideal for youngsters wanting to make extra money and who are prepared to do an early morning ride on their bicycles. Even for adults who have a moped and enjoy early mornings, this is a start to getting yourself on the feet again.

34. PARTY TAXI

Drinking and driving is a global problem. Take a problem and turn it into an opportunity. Offer a taxi service to take and fetch people to and from parties. Go in at a rate lower than the local taxis, but make sure you get a minimum number of people within the same area. There is nothing worse than going to an event and worrying about driving back. This is an untapped market and could bring in quite a good income. The downside is that it involves late night driving. However, if you are a night owl, then this is a great job. Take note that you have a bucket, or cleaning material on hand at all times in case you have someone that is too drunk! You should include a penalty fee/fine in your initial agreement for anyone that decides to puke in your car. This is a very pertinent issue and don't under-estimate it. Even if you check the passenger before they enter the car, you can never tell whether they may vomit or not.

35. PARTY BUS

Do you have a small bus or van? How about converting this into a traveling bar? You pick up small groups of people and have a bar in the bus. Depending on the size of the vehicle you can even have a barman serving drinks. All you do is drive around the city, stop at a few scenic spots as to allow for 'relief' breaks and then drop them back at the pick-up point later in the evening. This has become popular in some cities and I know of one person that started with a small mini van that could take 5 people. Today he has a full double decker bus and is part of the tourist attraction in his city.

36. PARTS SPECIALIST

The parts industry is where the money is! Whether a bicycle, motor cycle and car; this is a huge industry. There a thousands of second hand dealers and mechanics that are needing parts on a daily basis. Who offers the best deals and back-up service. Where can one get the best quality and warranties? Who specialises in which parts? Many car enthusiasts and restored and fixed many cars and already built up an extensive knowledge on parts dealers in their city. Imagine you could take this hobby a step further and gain extensive knowledge into who supplies which parts and what prices, and then offer the garages, workshops and dealers a service where you source the best deal on parts. You can either charge a handling fee or have a deal with the suppliers that they pay you a commission. Bottom line, anyone can phone you and save hours of phoning around time by getting the best deal through you.

37. PERSONALISED SIGHT SEEING SERVICE

In most cities you have to be a registered tour guide to offer tours. As someone that has worked in over 165 countries, I have yet to see a tour guide that hasn't been brain-washed to regurgitate council regulated information to tourists. If you are good at networking and marketing, nothing is stopping you advertising your services as a private guide where you offer to take couples around your city and show them how the 'normal' people live and where the locals shop. In other words, a non-tourist sight seeing service. Of course you can show the popular sights too. However, the focus is on personalised service and catering to the tourists whims. Charge a basic daily rate and treat them well and the tips can be very good.

38. PHOTO/POSTER DEALER

Many people are obsessed with cars and have posters of high performance vehicles in their den. If you are a keen photographer, how about taking photos of various interesting cars and creating posters of them? With digital printing this is very easy to do today and you can print from 1 to 10 posters. So you can keep collections 'exclusive.' Alternatively find nice frames and offer a framed collection of cars that you have photographed. You would advertise this in car enthusiast magazines. If you already have a camera, your initial cost to start this is virtually non existent. Where would you source cars to photograph? At various car exhibitions, races and rallies. I would however ask for permission from the owner before I photograph and sell pictures of one-off vehicles.

39. PUNCTURE REPAIR SERVICE

You can decide whether to specialise in car tires, motor cycles tires or bicycle wheels. Many people do not have the time to there vehicle or bike into a repair centre. Thus offer a home repair service. The market could be good for house-wives and elderly who need a puncture repaired. Most home DIY stores have DIY puncture repair kits for cars. It consists of a cork screw looking device that you thread a red rubbery strip through and push this into the inflated wheel where the hole/

puncture is. It then seals the tire without even having to take the wheel off the car. This could take you less than 10 minutes. The same is available for motor cycle wheels. Of course bicycle wheels can take a little longer to repair. You work out a price accordingly and start by advertising via leaflets through post boxes in your suburb. You will be surprised at the demand there is for this service.

40. RALLY/RACE ORGANISER

If you love organising and have a huge network of contacts, here is a great home based career; organise motor-cycle or bicycle rallies and races. You basically put everything together from the route to the marketing of the event as well as bringing in sponsorship. You would make your money from registration fees and sponsorship advertising and involvement. You could even supply the food and drinks for the refreshment stops along the way, or rent out these opportunities. Again, the sky is the limit.

41. ROUTE CO-ORDINATOR

Most, if not every company that provides transport of any sort has an individual that works out the routes involved. One cannot just get in a car and decide on the spur of the moment which route to take to a destination. For companies various factors play a roll that affect costs. Which is the shortest route? Does this involve more traffic than taking the highway? Long term, which route uses more fuel and creates more wear & tear on the vehicle. Does time of the day affect the amount of traffic and hence duration of trip? A specialist person is employed by most companies to assist with co-ordinating all routes taken by all transport. Often it is not a full time job and thus this person usually doubles as an administrative assistant. However, offering this service as an outsider for a specific fee per route can become a lucrative business once various companies start employing your skills. You will obviously need a good background knowledge of costs involved with running various vehicles as well as the demographics of the area you will be planning the routes.

42. SCHOOLCHILDREN DRIVING SERVICE

You will need an impeccable CV and character record, plus the correct license and insurances. However, if you can offer a 'Mom's Taxi' service driving kids to school and back, plus to extra mural activities in the afternoons – you have a small goldmine. However, you are asking parents to trust you with their children, so your driving skills, moral values and character needs to be squeaky clean.

43. SERVICE AT CLIENT'S HOME

As life becomes busier, it becomes more inconvenient to take your car in for a service. Many companies do not offer courtesy cars, so it really does mess around your daily routine. Years ago while living in the UK I remember owning an old Ford Escort and a mechanic did home repairs and services. Fair enough, most newer vehicles need a computer to analyse problems, but many older vehicles are fairly easy to service and do a plugs, filter and oil change. If you have knowledge of cars and can do this kind of service, advertise in your area that you will come out and do it. Work out a basic cost per car. Get a good deal on the parts and then do at at the person's home. The demand will be big and it's a great career to start off as a weekend job.

44. SMALL REMOVALS

In essence, this is very much like the furniture removal job, except that you move smaller items. I good distinction would be to consider the small items as anything you can carry on your own. This would include TV's, small drawer sets, chairs, etc. Here you would use a regular smaller panel van and run the business on your own. Do not underestimate smaller removals. Most people look at this as an 'annoyance' and not as profitable as moving big furniture. This may be so, however there are many people who require exactly this 'smaller' service. So it's a niche market that you can become busy in very quickly. It's particularly suited to a densely populated inner city environment.

45. STUNT PERFORMER

Some motor cycle, or bicycle riders just have the knack to do clever stunts on their bikes. Please note - I am not advocating any dangerous moves here. However, there may be some of you that simply have a knack to do weird and wonderful tricks on and with your bikes. If you have indeed practiced such things over the years, offer to do demonstrations and fairs, festivals and outdoor events, you will be amazed at the opportunities and the money that can be earned. Start by approaching organisers of such events and show them what you can do. Let your skill sell itself. Although, don't try be an 'Evil Knievel'!

46. TAXI SERVICE

You will need a valid driver's license and a suitable car. If this is something that interests you, start it on the side and let people know you can pick up and fetch as a reasonable rate. As you are competing with established companies, you may have to go in at a lower rate than the competition in order to get going. Initially you should look at your friends and social circle with your marketing and build it up from there. Airport transfer services are also very much in demand from the suburb to the airport in bigger cities.

47. TRAILER HIRE

A trailer is one of those items that isn't a good investment, unless you use it regularly. Think about it, how many people do you know with trailers, and the trailer is parked in the drive way or back yard for most of the year? Every time they want to use it, they have to pump up the tires! A trailer is way more economical to hire when you need it. I know a few people who started this service and are booked out every day. A trailer is easy to maintain, not much can go wrong with it and everyone collects it from your place of storage and brings it back again. Also, the cost to get started isn't that high either.

48. USE YOUR SPARE CAR FOR DRIVING SERVICES
Maybe you have a spare car, or are even prepared to use your main vehicle and offer short run taxi services and airport transfers. The airport transfer service is huge and daily there are hundreds of business people that make use of such a service. If you start with one or two routes at a competitive rate, you can very soon build up a big business.

49. VEHICLE SIGNAGE & ACCESSORIES
I removed the letters of my vehicle name and model type off my back bonnet of my car. These I replaced with my website address – suddenly I have a company car and a subtle classy moving advert. Some people may even enjoy adding a chrome stick on word under the model number so that everyone thinks they have a 'new' version of that car. For example in a $1 shop I found a plastic chrome finish adhesive word, "Exclusiv." (Yes it was spelt without the 'e' at the end!) I had just bought a C220 Mercedes and removed the C220 and replaced it with the 'Exclusiv' wording. Everyone stopped me and asked me which model this was. My friends who knew what I did, all wanted an "Exclusiv" label as well! Hence I figured, when I see something unique like this I will buy up the stock – especially when it's only $1 each! Find out who the suppliers are and start selling off unique signage and accessories; this can be for cars and bikes. Not many people do this anymore, and if you are looking for a low start-up exclusive side-line business, this is a good option.

50. WEDDING CAR HIRE BUSINESS

So you own a nice exclusive vehicle! Every thought of hiring it out for weddings or school balls? That Rolls Royce sitting in the garage for Sunday drives, but hasn't been driven in years? Now is the time to make money with it. In fact any exotic or different car can be offered out for hire. You drive it so you keep the control and also offset the maintenance costs of the vehicle, plus put some money in your pocket too!

When the going gets tough...
the tough hang in there.

Opportunities are never lost...
they are taken by others.

Don't let someone who gave up on their
dreams talk you out of yours.

YOUR OWN TRANSPORT HOME BUSINESS IDEAS

PERSONAL SERVICE & TREATMENTS AT HOME

Here are 50 ideas for businesses you can run from your home if you have a spare room/garage available. Once you build up a name, you can extend onto your home and even grow these businesses. Naturally some of them can also moved away from the home once you become established. Others, again allow you to travel and offer the services at the homes of clients. All in all here is a good general base of business ideas which you can start from home.

1. ASTROLOGY/TAROT/REIKI

The esoteric movement is incredibly popular today. More and more people are moving over to alternative medicine and treatment. This is a huge market and growing at a rapid rate. Every second magazine is offering courses on many new age topics. A basic knowledge can be learnt pretty quickly. Now you can offer these services to others. Couple this with good people skills and you can have a booming business in no time.

2. BUY AND SELL ANTIQUES

You need to know what you are doing here. I doubt you are going to learn this from any books or over the Internet within a few weeks. This has to be something you have been doing for years and have a keen interest and eye. Some countries have aired many interesting TV shows about specialists seeking out items in people's homes. Best of all, priceless antiques can be found in any country and city, especially at auctions and fairs. There are many people with a keen interest in antique items. Join various associations and make it known that you deal in specific items, and build your name in this way.

3. BED & BREAKFAST

The kids are out of the home and suddenly you have two extra bedrooms! Why not convert these into two suites with separate entrances and advertise your home as a bed & breakfast? Naturally you will have to check out the local regulations and become a licensed establishment. The focus needs to be on clean, safe and easily accessible environment where business people can feel at home. You may be near a sports complex where parents are looking for a safe place for their children to stay over. The options are huge. Yes, there is a cost involved to re-model existing rooms, but in the long-term this can bring in a regular income. Advertise at local companies, associations and on the Internet. Join local hospitality associations to find out the latest trends in the industry.

4. BOOK KEEPING SERVICE

My mom used to do this and help my dad that was an accountant. Obviously you will need a basic knowledge of accounting, but do not need to be a qualified CA. Here you help people get their books in order. There records are in a mess – and you sort it out. That's basically the nitty gritty of it! With so many small and medium enterprises starting up in the world today, more and more people need help getting their book in order. It is easy enough to run from home. Have your clients drop their papers by you, and you sort it out and reconcile everything for them at a fee.

5. BONSAI TREES

I know a number of people that have started home nurseries and it is a good business, especially if you love gardening. However, it can grow very quickly and become very time consuming. Somewhat less stress, and less popular would be to grow and sell bonsai trees. It is an art and needs to be learnt. The Internet is full of books and course that can teach you all about the art of growing bonsai trees. Today with apartments becoming more popular in build up cities, people are looking for unique plants to add some life to the concrete block they live in. What could be more novel and beautiful than a small bonsai tree! Start by doing a mail drop at various apartment buildings once you have a good stock of trees.

6. CANDLE-MAKING & SUPPLIES

Have you seen what candles cost in the stores today? Years ago I would have said that this was a low profit business. Today the tables have turned. Candles have become increasingly popular, not only in restaurants, but among families at social occasions as well. There are tons of books and course available on the Internet and this is a skill that is fairly easy to learn. In fact the more creative you are, the better! It is recommended that you have a supply of standard candles for people with lower budgets, but then also your own special candles that become associated with your brand, at a higher price.

Once the business starts growing, you can offer to supply materials to other candle-makers as well as offer courses to people wanting to learn the art.

7. CATERING SERVICE

Yes, this is an old idea; nothing new here! However, every body must eat. There are always parties happening everywhere. Companies and individuals constantly have functions throughout the year. Often I have heard people say that this market is saturated, yet every year new companies appear and become successful. It's all about the quality of your food and the value that you offer. Why not offer a different menu to what's out there? Present your food in a novel way; think out of the box! Every city has tons of restaurants, some make it, some don't! It's the novel ones that make it; learn from them! You will need your own cutlery and crockery; buy this from a catering wholesale store and make sure to include a 'breakage deposit' at all events.

8. CHILD MINDING/BABYSITTING SERVICE

Offer to look after other people's children at your own home. Set an age group with which you are comfortable and let word of mouth build up your business. As it grows, you may need to have your home inspected by the relevant authorities and register your business. As it grows you could even employ people to do most of the work while you supervise them. Just bear in mind that when working with other people's children, your will have to thoroughly screen people you employ.

9. DEBT COUNSELLING

Some people just cannot work with money and are hopeless at organising their finances. If you have good skills in money management, this could be an ideal opportunity for you. You can approach banks and companies and even local NGO's to offer your services.

10. DIAPER SALES

Besides the facts that babies are born every day, there are many elderly and incontinent adults that need diapers. When last have you look at the cost of diapers at the supermarket? I remember when our kids were babies, we found a wholesale supply from a lady who did this from home. Find a supplier and besides advertising on a 'Craig's List' type site, you can put a simple notices on notice boards at shopping malls; no high tech needed here as many moms walk past these notice boards. What about diapers for the elderly? Simply advertise your better value, cheaper diapers at old age homes to get you going.

11. DRESSMAKING & FASHION CLOTHES

Do you have a sewing machine that is collecting dust? Do you enjoy sewing? Just look at the prices of new clothes today, and if that isn't an incentive, nothing will get you going! Sewing classes are readily available, and dress patterns are easily obtained from many stores and magazines. Creating the professional look is relatively easy with today's sewing machines, books and ideas on the Internet. Start by making your own clothes with your own designs. Your family and friends will soon notice, and want the same. Remember to always sew a tag with your name, address & website into each garment you make. This will bring in re-orders.

12. ETIQUETTE COURSES

We have all heard the elderly comment that the youth of today don't have manners. In fact, when was last time you saw a man stand up when a woman enters the room? How about starting a finishing school for girls, or a simple general course in etiquette and manners aimed at men? Again, you can find all the info you need on the Internet. Target upmarket areas where parents have the money to send their children to such courses. Offer you program to schools and colleges. There will always be a market.

13. FANCY DRESS HIRE

Although many party shops have cheap fancy dress costumes, many people still prefer hiring outfits for special events. Research has shown that anywhere between the 2nd and 3rd hire you have made your costs back on the outfit and from then it's pure profit. This is something you can run from the spare bedroom or garage. If you are skilled with a sewing machine, then you can even make most of the outfits on your own. You do need to take dry cleaning costs into consideration. Ideally make the outfits in such a way that they can easily be washed at home as well. Although adult themed outfits are good, children's outfits are cheaper to produce and buy and would be the market that is more active. To cover accidental damage or theft, you need to ask for a refundable deposit that covers the cost of the clothing. I know a lady in a neighbouring suburb that started small and has now been doing this for over 20 years. She has a great steady income and a big supply of outfits and runs the business half days. Start by advertising at schools and party shops, plus the Internet.

14. FACIAL COSMETICS, HAND CREAMS AND BODY LOTIONS

My mom hand a moisturising cream recipe left to her by her father (my grandfather). The ingredients are all natural. Then again there are many factory wholesale stores which will sell you creams, soaps and skin products in bulk and for wholesale prices. All you need to do is source nice containers and put your own label onto this, and suddenly you have your own skin range! Start by sharing it with friends and get them to spread the word. Try and focus on organic products which have not been tested on animals; that's a good selling point.

15. FITNESS (YOGA) CLASSES

Learn to become a yoga teacher. They say that a supple spine will keep you younger longer – that alone is a good reason to start doing yoga. You can offer these classes at home for the surrounding people in your street. Once it build up you can offer to do classes at your local gym. Also make sure the room you use at home is well ventilated, a comfortable temperature and clean.

16. FENG SHUI SERVICE

Feng Shui has become immensely popular in the last few years and there are dozens of books available on the subject. To learn the basic principles is fairly easy to do and shouldn't take you more than a few weeks. Now you can offer your services to corporate companies, professionals and home owners, helping all to balance the environment they work/live in.

17. FRAME AND SELL COLLECTIONS FOR DISPLAY

This is a nice home business for a creative individual. Yes you can initially lay out some money for framing equipment, but I would suggest you start off by taking your products to a framer first and build up the business. Everyone collects all sorts of stuff, so keep an eye out for unique coin collections, stamps, autographed pictures, antiques, replica gadgets, insects and anything that can be framed. Now start a new trend a 'collector' frames items and start selling these.

18. FUNKY BUTTONS

Yes, I know that the silly buttons people wear are corny. But guess what, many people wear them and they are popular at conferences, outings, events, bazaars, concerts and many more functions. Guess what? Someone is making them and making money! Is it you? A button machine is fairly inexpensive and you could even sell them to novelty stores, sports clubs and schools. Make up a button around a current event, or even a silly saying. Have your kids wear it to school and get their friends to buy them. You can basically put any picture or and wording on them. The sky is the limit.

19. GIFT BASKETS

Have you ever looked around at at the variety of gift baskets available in shops? Dare I presume that there wasn't much of a variety. The norm is a bottle of champagne (alcoholic and/or non alcoholic) some dried fruits and nuts and maybe a cute small teddy bear. If anything I dread receiving gift baskets as Thank You gifts at conferences, as half the contents I don't eat, and the rest is most nonsense. Here is really big market if you have a creative flair, and contacts for buying quality items at good prices.

Compile practical gift baskets for industry specific companies, i.e. approach IT companies have a specific gift basket for them that includes a memory stick, computer screen cleaning material, utility bag for cables, etc. Every industry can have a selection specific gift baskets. Approach companies in your area with your offerings.

20. GROW AND SELL YOUR OWN VEGETABLES
Do you live on a small holding? Or maybe even have a large back garden that hasn't been put to use. One of the most relaxing hobbies around is gardening. So why not put this to good use and plant a herb or a vegetable garden. Do some research on seasons to grown particular vegetables in. Work on a turn around time and offer to sell this from your home. Nothing beats a nice home grown lettuce or fresh lemon grass grown in your own pot. With careful planning you could quite easily build up a very profitable business in a short period of time. Start out by approaching your neighbours and friends. As the business grows you can put up a greenhouse and have your own special packaging. The sky is the limit!

21. HANDWRITING ANALYSIS
Don't be misled, hand-writing analysis is a proven science and many companies use the services of these experts to check out prospective employees. Police have also been known to seek guidance on analysing criminals through their hand writing. Many people want one-on-one consultations and have their own hand writing analysed. There

are many books available on the subject, as well as courses on the Internet. If you do this already, great! If not, it is fairly inexpensive to get started, it just takes time to study everything and practice it on family and friends. Once you are proficient at it, then you make your services known to companies, local law enforcement as well as your social circle. The accuracy of your analysis will determine your popularity.

22. HEALTH CONSULTANT

Courses in reflexology, acupuncture, osteopathy, iridology, homeopathy etc. are offered in every major city. Take a course that interests you and get your certification. You could initially start with an established practitioner to get experience and see how the business runs, and then slowly do it from your own home by converting a spare room into a consulting room. This type of service is becoming increasing popular in suburbs today.

23. HERB GARDEN

Herbs are becoming more popular by the day for flavouring foods and for natural health remedies. However, not all supermarkets have a wide range of herbs. If you have specialist knowledge of herbs, it is a great idea to grow them in your own back garden, and then offer them for sale to certain supermarkets, health foods stores and individuals who use them. You don't need much space and again, there are many good informative books available in most libraries and on the Internet. You could even begin arranging regular meetings at home where you educate your clients on the uses of the various herbs.

24. HOME BAKING

If you enjoy baking, why don't you sell your goodies? Cake shops, company do's, events, schools, churches etc. all need cakes and cookies. Children's birthday parties are a huge market if you can make cartoon cakes and cakes around well known children's characters. Have you been into a mainstream store recently and seen the prices they charge for such cakes. You will find hundreds of ideas on the Internet and can star small with a regular stove, eventually building up to more professional equipment.

25. HAIRDRESSING SERVICE /NAIL STUDIO

My neighbour is a hairdresser and works from home. Plus she does nails. And don't laugh, recently she did a course in 'anal' bleaching! Don't even go there! I laughed when I heard about this, but she is laughing all the way to the bank; people are coming to her for this! From 08h00 in the morning there is always a car in the driveway and she has a handful of regular clients. Over the years she has kitted out an entire salon in a spare room and today makes a great income from home.

26. HOME MADE HONEY OR JAM

When last did you look at the price of home-made jams and honey in the supermarket. You are paying premium price for these products, and most of the time they are not true home made, but just cleverly packaged. Firstly you need to find a reliable supplier of glass jars and learn/know how to make jams. Start small through family and friends and build it up from there. Maybe even supplying your surrounding supermarkets with the 'genuine' product!

27. HOME MADE SAUCES

In a similar vein, how about making your own sauces? From barbecue sauces to marinades. If you have a particularly good mix which friends have always raved about – why not turn this into a business? Obviously a good knowledge of food hygiene and preparation is essential. I have personally seen how a friend's home made barbecue sauce has become a national brand within 5 years. The possibilities are endless!

28. HYPNOTHERAPY

I cannot stress the importance of having an accredited qualification in hypnotherapy. Don't just go on any course – you really need some medical and psychological insight here. Hypnotherapy is becoming increasingly popular due to it being non invasive. However, you need to know what you are doing. If you want to be successful in this business, word of mouth and your reputation are the only things that will ring you clients. Remember that you have to compete with a fairly bad entertainment image of hypnotherapy where people think you will do weird things to them while they are 'under'. Hence the importance of professionalism and correct accreditation.

The market is huge, from losing weight to stopping smoking. Many people have fears and issues about many things. Your market is huge. You can even create downloadable mp3's that patients can listen to at home and buy off the Internet. The market is huge.

29. IMAGE CONSULTANT

Have you noticed that some people just look good, no matter what they wear? It's as if they have an eye for mixing and matching clothes, make-up and apparel. I have a daughter like that – she chooses the clothes for all of us! Professional people need to look good and create the right impressions. Just take a walk through any city or shopping mall, how many people are well dressed and wearing something that suits them perfectly? And don't make the mistake of thinking that 'well-dressed' refers to expensive and tailor-made clothing! Not at all, it's merely about combining your clothes properly and knowing what styles suit you. Offer an image service and teach people to wear what suits them. When they leave people will comment on their looks; that's all the referral marketing you need to build your business.

30. INKJET REFILL SERVICE

It's cheaper to buy a new printer today than it is replacement cartridges. In many cities inkjet refill businesses have shot up, but mostly in shopping malls and commercial areas. Thus there is nice market in the suburbs supplying people in your neighbourhood. It's not that difficult to learn and one buys the ink in bulk and the returns are really good. Today printer companies have put chips on the cartridges to prevent refilling. However, now one can buy chip 're-setters' as well which now make the business viable again.

31. IRONING SERVICE

Who likes ironing? Believe it or not, some people do. With todays rushed life-style no one has the time to iron. If you can offer a fair priced service with a 12hour turn-around – I guess you could keep yourself busy every single day. Especially if you live in a built up area with many apartments around you. This is even a job you can run out of your own apartment. Simply begin by advertising your service to those around you... and make sure you have a really good iron. As the business grows you can invest in a bigger press and take on more orders.

32. KEY FINDING SERVICE

With today's crime rate, losing a key can be a traumatic experience. Becoming a locksmith is a trade on its own. There is another simpler solution and that is to sell keyring holders to people which states, "If found, please drop at your nearest post box. We will pay the postage". Each keyring has a unique number printed on it so that you can source the owner of the key. The initial cost of the keyring covers postage and phone calls to track down the owner. You can have a whole range of key rings with this message printed on it.

33. KNITTING FOR MONEY

I have a sister in law that started a home knitting business, from scarves to jerseys. Within a few months she had bought a machine which would do any design and within a few years she had an extension built on the house, employed people part time and owned a number of machines. They approached schools, sports clubs, companies and people in the vicinity and soon they couldn't keep up anymore. They always kept their prices fair, used good quality wool and tailor made each piece of clothing.

34. MAKE-UP FOR ANY OCCASION

Niche markets are often very good to be in. However, a product or service that most people need, tends to guarantee a regular constant income. Have you completed a make-up course? Are you good at doing make-up? Do you have an eye for what kind of make-up suits a particular person? From weddings, graduation ceremonies, special occasions to fancy dress parties. The scope is HUGE and the potential massive. If you can make someone look good, plus make them feel special in the process, that's   pretty much half the battle won. If you don't have a spare room at home to convert into a salon, you can start by applying make-up in your kitchen or lounge. This is an ideal small start-up business which can build into a busy enterprise simply by starting through word-of-mouth.

35. MASSEUR, MASSEUSE OR CHIROPODIST

Once again, courses are plenty and with a bit of effort you can get your qualification and then run your business from home. This is a business suited for a people's person and someone who enjoys helping others. Start with friends and social circle.

36. MATERNITY DRESS BUSINESS

The majority of women have babies, very few couples decide to remain single parents. Thus the baby market is huge. Maternity dresses is a specialised market and most women either throw away or pack away their maternity dresses when they are finished having children. Hence can you imagine the market for second hand maternity dress business. Buy good quality dresses and have them dry cleaned and offer them for a good deal. You could start including a whole range of baby products, including prams, toys, nappy's and baby clothes. Initially you can advertise in family and bridal magazines and in local newspapers in suburbs that attract your couples.

37. MOM'S TAXI

I have a huge respect and new understanding of this title since my wife has been driving our daughters around to every possible extra mural activity after school. If it isn't gymnastics, then its music lessons. From there it's off to Kumon maths and then rehearsal for the school play. It doesn't stop! Now every other mother around does the same thing. Imagine the amount of damage to the environment, cost of fuel, etc. Start a mom's taxi service in your street or suburb for a fee and fill the car with children on the same route as your own. Alternatively as this build up you can actually start a 'mom's taxi' with your own mini bus.

38. MULTI-LEVEL MARKETING

Please understand that a legal multi-level marketing company is NOT a pyramid scheme. Today many high profile companies are moving to the multi-level marketing route as this is very much part of a future trend. The social media such as Twitter has made many companies nervous as everyone is tweeting about everybody, everything and every company. Today, before we buy, we see what has been said on the social media, and we ask our friends. Therefore network marketing is growing in popularity.

However, not all MLM companies are the same. Find one with a product that you believe in. Also, and most importantly, realise that this is a full-time 24/7 job. Unfortunately many of these companies have unrealistic marketing strategies and rely on people's greed to get them to sign up. Understand right here and now that it is NOT as easy as they make it out to be and that if you only spend an hour a week doing the job, it is going to bring in very little, if any money. MLM is like any business, you need to invest time and build a solid downline. Only if you are prepared to do this, you should look at various companies out there.

39. PET SITTING

So you like animals and have a large property! Here's a great opportunity! Most animals prefer a back yard to a kennel. Keep a limit on the number of pets you accept and really spend time with the animals. Pet owners would much rather leave their animals with someone that pays special attention. Plus you can offer to take in a variety of animals, from tortoises to birds. The sky is the limit. I would like to know my pets are in safe hands when I am on holiday. Simply start by offering the service in your neighbourhood.

Alternatively, offer a trusted home feeding service. Some people may even not be comfortable with leaving their animals anywhere but at home. Make arrangements that you check on and feed their animals at their home. This could be a big market too! However, if you do grow big and need to employ people, make sure they are 100% trustworthy in other people's homes.

40. PRIVATE INVESTIGATOR

Don't confuse this with the dangerous escapades on TV series. People (including lawyers and spouses) need someone to keep an eye on other people activities and collect information. Some of this can be done by following their activities on social media – so you don't even need to leave the house. Investigating activities of others is way less dangerous than looking for murderers! Offer your services by advertising on the Internet and spreading the word amongst your social circle. It is up to you to accept a job or not, therefore you are always in control of any risk element that may come with the job.

41. PARTY PLANNER FOR PERFUMES, COSMETICS, JEWELLERY, ADULT AND GIFT ITEMS

So, you are a social animal? You know plenty of people and love organising parties? Find a nice product that you enjoy and either host your own parties, or offer to host parties for people looking to do this themselves, but don't have a large social circle.

42. RESTAURANT FROM HOME

Do you like cooking? How about offering an exclusive night out for 6 – 10 people. You may be from another country living in an area that is not used to your food. Offer an exquisite foreign experience for the locals. Decorate the dining area accordingly, inform the people about your culture and history and make it a super night out! Or consider having various theme nights for people in your neighbourhood. You can even offer exclusive dinners to company executives for their out of town visitors. Just think of something novel and couple it with a great experience and great food.

43. SELF IMPROVEMENT CLASSES

You can teach individuals or small groups of people at home and cover topics such as weight loss, self confidence, goal setting and basically anything that leads to a person improving their self image. You will need to be an inspirational type person yourself and do some research and attend similar course. You can purchase a license from a well-known trainer and offer their material, or you can design your own courses. Word of mouth will dictate the success of this venture. Focus on individual attention and really giving value. You need to care about the welfare of others and really help guide them towards their goals, then success must follow.

44. SEWING ALTERATIONS SERVICE

This is very different from making clothes and the market is huge. Many people still have clothes in mint condition and need some minor alteration done, from lengthening trouser legs to taking in the waist. If you are talented in this area and can work neatly, this is a great home business to get into. Think about it, in your family alone, how many items of clothing need alteration? Have I made my point?

45. SEX AIDS & LINGERIE PARTIES

This is something suited to a lady and aimed at ladies. The sex industry has build up a bad name for itself and no self-respecting woman wants to walk into a sex store in a red-light area and look for 'toys' on her own. Europe is more liberal and has stores in better areas, but in general this seems to be a problem world-wide. So why not start a home party type of event where you can invite ladies over for a cheese and wine, and show/demo the various outfits and toys you have for sale. You will need to be outgoing and not shy and offer a tasteful selection of products.

This may not be for everyone, but you do need to realise that although many people don't speak about the subject, this alone opens up a huge opportunity to not only sell products, but offer a safe environment for people to chat about and also listen to advice on sexuality. You could take this far further than just supplying products, but offering simple ideas and advice as well by having guest speakers attending your events too. If you can build trust and create a fun event, I would think that this can become huge. In fact I know of one friend who is a lawyer, who's wife started this as a sideline business, and he started helping her in the end; it went massive.

46. SPECIAL INTEREST GROUPS

You may have an interest in a specialist field. Find people with a similar interest and arrange regular meetings. These can be once a month or once per week, and you arrange everything. Maybe there is a movie they need to see, research that has to be done, etc. You supply your home as the venue, arrange the food, drinks and setting at a fee per event, or per head. Alternatively you can approach smaller groups struggling to find a venue and also offer to do their admin and phoning of members to remind them of meetings. You charge for all of this. Alternatively, you start a specialist club and charge a membership fee that covers all these costs! You could even offer your home to smaller support groups who need a venue. The scope is fairy large here.

47. SWEETS & CHOCOLATES

Have you ever bought Belgian chocolates? If not, it's like buying an expensive perfume in a high street store. It's expensive and comes wrapped in an exquisite box. I have often wondered if it isn't the packaging that makes my mind believe that the perfume smells so good! If you are talented in the kitchen, why not create your own exclusive range of sweets and chocolates. As much, if not more time needs to be spent of the packaging and marketing. Of course you must only use the best ingredients and ideally 'organically' grown products only. Focus on detail and taste, while also extending the sensory experience to the packaging. Market your sweets and chocolates over the Internet, to exclusive stores and to selected brand conscious friends. Humans have been conditioned to be brand conscious; watch how everyone will suddenly want your products!

48. TATTOO SERVICE

There are a number of training courses available and tattoos are becoming increasingly popular. The start-up costs are not that extreme and you basically need a spare room in you home to start the business. Having an artistic flair and getting on well with others will definitely help boost the business.

49. TUTOR SERVICE

Are you an ex teacher? Do you have knowledge of various school subjects? From maths to geography to languages.!Advertise after hours tutoring to schools in your area and make sure you know what is required in the current syllabus. Due to the current state of the education system world-wide, many youngsters are in need of help. If you enjoy kids and teaching – this is something to consider.

50. WEDDING PLANNER

If you love organising events and can handle the emotions of a bride; then this is the job for you. The wedding industry is MASSIVE! People are getting married every day! If you are attentive and give the bride a special experience and take all the stress away from her; you have it made. Advertise at wedding venues, on the Internet, in publications and the newspaper. Just the bride recommending you to her friends will build your business if you give her an unforgettable wedding.

YOUR OWN PERSONAL HOME SERVICE BUSINESS IDEAS

PUBLIC SEMINARS & KEYNOTES

Would you like Wolfgang to speak at your
organisations next meeting or event?
Simply visit www.wolfgangriebe.com
for more details and keynotes on offer.

MORE INSPIRATIONAL VIDEOS ON YOU TUBE

Subscribe to Wolfgang's You Tube Channel, https://www.youtube.com/
user/inspiringtheworld
for hundreds of inspirational and entertaining videos.

HARD COPY PRINTED BOOKS

All Wolfgangs's publication are available in Paperback and hardcover.
Visit www.wolfgangriebe.com, or the publisher at
www.mindpowerpublications.com, or most book suppliers online

ABOUT THE AUTHOR:

Wolfgang Riebe is a globally acclaimed magical keynote speaker who has inspired millions with his mesmerising performances and motivational speeches. A towering figure in both the magic and speaking industries, he is a best-selling author of over 60 books on magic, business, and inspiration. With over 30 years of experience, Wolfgang has captivated audiences in more than 165 countries, from Hollywood to Singapore, and has starred in over 200 television shows, including his own prime-time series.

Wolfgang's journey began in South Africa, and he has since lived in the UK, Germany, and Switzerland. In 2012, he earned his Certified Speaking Professional (CSP) designation from the National Speakers Association in America, a prestigious honour held by fewer than 750 speakers worldwide at the time. He made history as the first two-term national president of the Speakers Association for Africa and has shared his insights as a TEDx speaker. His groundbreaking research culminated in his acclaimed book, "Complexity Simplified," which has been cited by over 300 doctoral students.

Wolfgang's adventures are as diverse as his achievements. From walking with penguins in Antarctica to exploring the Arctic icecap and surviving force 12 hurricanes, he has lived a life that most can only dream of. His books reflect his passion for sharing his wisdom and helping others find meaning in their lives. Wolfgang embodies the KISS principle, believes in the magic of life, celebrates milestones, and charts paths to future success. He is a rare speaker who practices what he preaches and truly walks his talk, making him a world leader in his field.

DISCOVER YOUR MAGIC

BEST SELLER!　　　　　　　　　　　　　　**BEST SELLER!**

7 STEPS TO A TRULY FULFILLING LIFE!

PRACTICAL LIFE SKILLS TO HELP YOU ACHIEVE YOUR DREAMS.

How to gain the competitive edge in your life & business. Become aware of everything around you. Clarify and achieve all your goals. Learn to adapt to change. Create a positive image with every one around you. Wolfgang has inspired and motivated more than a million people around the world. This is a comprehensive study on how to gain mastery over your own life, whether in the corporate, or personal field. Every aspect is clearly presented, without losing the true sense or heart of the matter. Wolfgang writes with the humility of someone who has gone deeply into the subject, and who has learnt through actual experience. An inspirational book to change your life.

✓ Understand the power of **logic** in achieving success.

✓ Techniques and skills to help build **awareness**.

✓ Real, usable & practical techniques to achieve **goals**.

✓ Creating & maintaining great first **impressions**.

✓ Embracing **change** and applying this in our fast changing business world.

✓ Foster & nurture business **associations**.

✓ The importance of **laughter** in coping with everyday life.

Now in it's 9th re-print and completely revised!

FULL ONLINE VIDEO COURSE ALSO AVAILABLE

HARD COVER: ISBN-13: 979-8531601575
PAPERBACK & PDF: ISBN-13: 978-1438215891
E-READER FORMATS: ISBN: 978-1458082886

LEADERSHIP SKILLS IN NETWORK MARKETING

DO YOU HAVE WHAT IT TAKES TO BE A SUCCESSFUL NETWORK MARKETER?

MLM TIPS & SKILLS TO BUILD YOUR DOWNLINE

Network marketing can be one of the most rewarding and lucrative careers in the world, as proven by thousands of people. However, there is way more to running a successful MLM business than simply recruiting a downline!

Why is it that so few people make such a huge success of such a simple concept? Simple! It's not a quick overnight 'get-rich-quick' scheme, but a professional business that needs to be run as such. You need to be a leader, manager, friend and mentor to your entire team, and lead by example.

Here's a practical book which shares with you various secrets and tips to building a successful multi-level marketing business

Is network marketing as easy as it sounds?

Leadership qualities of a good networker.

Would you like to be sponsored by you?

Women as network leaders.

Quick tips on being a successful leader.

HARD COVER: ISBN-13: 979-8531645395
PAPERBACK & PDF: ISBN-13: 978-1470085377
E-READER FORMATS: ISBN: 978-1466058248

POSITIVE THINKING
250 MOTIVATIONAL QUOTES

250 ORIGINAL QUOTATIONS
WITH PHOTO, EXPLANATION AND VIDEOS!

Enjoy a unique collection of 250 original quotes, reflections and thoughts to help you find direction and be more positive in life. As a keynote speaker, Wolfgang Riebe has inspired millions of people throughout the world and shared positive messages live on the platform, in his many publications and on social media.

This book is unique in that all motivational quotes, are accompanied by a photo and Wolfgang's explanation of each quotation and what it means to him. Numerous links to various Quick Tip videos accompany many of the quotes in order to share even more insights.

It's a first and current one-of-a-kind book of daily affirmations from a one-of-a-kind man whose vision it is to create memorable magical moments for everyone that crosses his path.

Perfect as a corporate gift to inspire clients and staff!
Great for the beside to read one quote before going to sleep.
Also ideal for waiting/reception rooms and as a coffee table book!

Available in Hard Cover, Paperback, PDF and all E-Reader formats

HARD COVER (FULL COLOUR): ISBN-13: 979-8548313478
PAPERBACK & PDF: ISBN-13: 978-1547291854
E-READER FORMATS: ISBN: 978-1370912896

SALES SECRETS & NEGOTIATION SKILLS

A BEGINNER'S GUIDE TO SALES & NEGOTIATION

In today's fast paced world all leaders and business people need a basic understanding of strategic sales and negotiation skills.

Here is a simply written and easy to understand book on the basics of sales and negotiation that can be read within a few hours, plus give you that much needed insight to close off the next deal.

SALES SECRETS:
9 Steps to successful sales.
Identify your target market & competitors.
Plan & future proof your business.
Learning about your customer's business.
Understanding the marketing process.
Preparing a sales presentation.
Face-to-face selling while listening.
Do the sell!
Feedback and focusing on the 2nd sale.
Follow-up regularly.

NEGOTIATION SKILLS:
The elements of negotiation.
The actual negotiation process.
General negotiation tips & ideas.

HARD COVER: ISBN-13: 979-8548498700
PAPERBACK & PDF: ISBN-13: 978-1451591781
E-READER FORMATS: ISBN: 978-1458010759

POTATO WEDGES FOR THE HEART

INSPIRATIONAL STORIES, THOUGHTS & INSIGHTS
THAT COULD CHANGE YOUR LIFE!

Chicken Soup of the Soul is a world best seller and phenomenal book! Well, here is it's brother... Potato Wedges from the Heart!

When you picture a potato wedge, what comes to mind? Something warm, tasty and cosy?

That's what this life-changing book is... a collection of short, tasty inspirational stories collected from all over the world, by unknown authors. They will not only touch your heart, but also feed your soul. Careful consideration and deep thought has gone into the selection of stories, insights and life lessons that are shared in this book. Wolfgang also shares his interpretation of all the thoughts shared, in order to expand on the meaning and give you real value from each story.

Most stories are only one page long, yet have so much depth that just reading one insight per day will give you a new meaning to life. All stories are expanded upon with many more anecdotes, personal experiences and quotations.

If you want to put your life back into perspective, be inspired, and find the magic within yourself again, this book could just the answer!

Great for the beside to read one story per night before going to sleep!

HARD COVER: ISBN-13: 979-8533154222
PAPERBACK & PDF: ISBN-13: 978-1489533258
E-READER FORMATS: ISBN: 978-1301031252

Made in the USA
Las Vegas, NV
28 January 2025

17148102R00131